Τὸ Εὐαγγέλιον
(The Good News)

Book Of Sermons

T0194140

By
Clyde C. Wilton

Order this book online at www.trafford.com
or email orders@trafford.com

Most Trafford titles are also available at major online book retailers.

Scripture quotations marked KJV are from the Holy Bible, King James Version
(Authorized Version). First published in 1611. Quoted from the KJV Classic
Reference Bible, Copyright © 1983 by The Zondervan Corporation.

Printed in the United States of America.

ISBN: 978-1-4907-5398-0 (sc)
ISBN: 978-1-4907-5399-7 (hc)
ISBN: 978-1-4907-5397-3 (e)

Trafford rev. 01/20/2015

 www.trafford.com

North America & international
toll-free: 1 888 232 4444 (USA & Canada)
fax: 812 355 4082

Preface

We are living in a great technological age. My life began when the horse and buggy days were phasing out and the horseless carriage was becoming popular in our United States of America. At that time, it was the Model T Ford car that gave America a new method of transportation.

During my youth, the telephone began to develop into the new art of communication over the wire. I remember that while I was a boy, we had a telephone about the size of a small suitcase that was nailed to the wall and was operated by two "B" batteries about the size of medium-sized pickle jars. My grandparents lived just about a half-mile to the west of our home. For awhile, communicating with my grandparents by phone was the extent of our communication system. However, at one point the telephone wire was stretched as far away as to my Uncle Jake's place, which was about 5 miles. That was quite an occasion, since there were also 4 other people who were hooked up on that line along the way.

The radio was also coming into use while I was growing up, but at that time the radios were very simple. One of my hobbies was to make "crystal set" radios, which were early, tubeless radio receivers. They were made my wrapping copper wire around a corncob and using a "cat whisker" contact with headphones. It was always a thrill to make a radio, and one time I even received a radio message from as far away as Old Mexico. For me, that was a great invention, but some were already talking about other fantastic inventions. Some were even speculating about sending a picture through the air, but most people knew that could never happen!

For the first 20 years of my life, I lived on a small farm with my family, which consisted of my parents, Elmer and Eula Wilton, and my older brothers, Luther Virgil (L.V.) and Anthony Wilton. Our farm was about 4 miles southeast of Jermyn, Texas and about 12 miles northwest of Jacksboro, Texas, and about midway between Wichita Falls, Texas and Fort Worth, Texas. Living on the farm was a lot of work, but we had plenty to eat, even during the Depression days. There were always the staples of black-eyed peas from the garden, milk from the cows, and eggs from the chickens.

My grade school education began at the Winn Hill Public School in the Winn Hill community, located about 2 miles down the road from our farm. It was a small, one-teacher schoolhouse with a total attendance of about 20 students, and it was close enough that I walked to school each day. Into my third year at Winn Hill, our school consolidated with the Jermyn Public School. After that, I rode a school bus each day to nearby Jermyn, Texas, and that was where I graduated from high school.

My parents were hard workers, and they usually worked from sunrise to sunset each day. They were not interested in reading, so we did not have a big library of books at home. In fact, our library consisted of one book, the King James Version of the Bible. At an early age, I learned to appreciate the Word of God.

After graduating from the Jermyn High School, I began attending college at Weatherford Jr. College in Weatherford, Texas. It was a great time in my life. For the first time, I could make my own decisions, and I thought that when I got an education, I would become a "big shot." Since it was a busy life, I no longer had time to go to church or read my Bible, or so I thought. But into my second year of college, something strange happened to me. My worldly lifestyle came to a dead-end street. I was forced to contemplate the question, "What is the purpose of life?"

I became obsessed with the idea that if this physical life is all there is, then there is nothing of eternal value. I cried out to God, but there was seemingly no way for me to communicate with Him. I was miserable for several days, and finally, I went back home to the farm. It was during that time that my lifestyle was changed, and the Lord revealed himself to me. I believed that God wanted me to proclaim the Gospel of Jesus the Christ. With His help, that is what I have been doing since March 1940.

Returning to college, I graduated from Howard Payne College in 1943. Later, I went to Southwestern Baptist Theological Seminary and graduated from the seminary in 1948. Following the seminary, I was the pastor of several churches, and then I served for twelve years in the U.S. Air Force as a chaplain. Following active military service, I was pastor of Emmanuel Baptist Church for 40 years, until 2007. I am now retired.

I believe in the Gospel of Jesus. It saved me and gave me a salvation that blesses me every day. I have seen, and still do every day, how it saves people who submit themselves to God. During my active preaching ministry, I spoke extemporaneously with sermon notes, but I seldom ever wrote out my sermons word for word. Now, I have prepared the full manuscripts for 25 of those sermons and have put them in book form, with the goal of extending my ministry.

My first sermon was delivered in 1940. The text was from Romans 1:16-17, which says, "For I am not ashamed of the gospel, for it is the power of God unto salvation to all who believe, the Jew first, then the Greek. For in it the righteousness of God has been revealed from faith to faith, as it has been written, 'The righteous shall live by faith.' "

The Gospel is for everyone, and it makes brothers and sisters out of enemies. It is the only message that is the same for all people. It is for the rich or the poor; it is for all races, whether white, yellow, brown, or black. There is no difference. It has been my privilege to share the gospel with the Indians in India; it has been the same with the Blacks and the Indians in Guyana, South America; and, it was my privilege to help establish a Christian Church with the Japanese in Japan. Yes, the Gospel has the power to save all who believe in the Lord Jesus the Christ.

I am eager to share the Gospel, because it is adequate even for those who are near death. When I was a pastor of the Baptist Church at Bellevue, Texas I was able to minister of an elderly man as he was leaving this earthly life. Rev. Neeley was a retired Baptist minister who was 92 years old. One cold December day just after Christmas, Bro. Neeley called me and asked me to come to his house. I went there and we sat around his wood stove in his living room. He told me that he did not think that he would have the opportunity of telling the church about his experience, so he wanted me to tell them. He said that the Lord was so close to him that he could almost touch his garment. His brother-in-law said that on Christmas day he had passed into a state of glory and that he was in love with everyone.

Bro. Neeley asked me to read Psalm 116. I read the chapter in his presence, and at the reading of verse 15, "Precious in the sight of the Lord is the death of his saints," he burst out in a loud shout of Joy. I have never seen anyone so happy. He was not sick, and he appeared to me to be in excellent health. That was about noontime. In the afternoon, he laid down to take a nap, and the Lord took him about 2:00 p.m. I shared that testimony to the church, and I have shared it each year with each church I have been associated with. That was in 1948, so I have told it more than 60 times. It has been an encouragement to me over the years.

It is exciting to see people's lives changed when they receive the power of the saving message of Jesus. So, if these sermons can help the lost sinner find his way to eternal life, my goal will be accomplished. May God's blessings be on all who read them!

Τὸ Εὐαγγέλιον
The Good News

Amazing Grace
(Ephesians 2:1-10)

One of the great hymns of all time, Amazing Grace, was composed by John Newton, who was one of the greatest sinners of his time. Indeed, the grace that could save a wretched man like John Newton was grace that was amazing.

John had many problems in his life before he experienced the grace of God. He had a wonderful mother who taught him verses of the Bible and introduced him to the hymns of the church. John was a young boy when his mother died, but he remembered her tearful prayers for him. As John grew older, he wandered away from his mother's teaching and became a very wicked man.

When Paul wrote to Timothy (1 Timothy 1:2), he said, "...to Timothy my true son in the faith: grace, mercy and peace from God our Father and Christ Jesus our Lord." Paul used the three blessings of grace, mercy, and peace together in one greeting. The **grace** Paul spoke of was the Greek word, χαρίς (charis). This describes God's attitude toward the lawbreaker and the rebel, because the grace of God always comes before mercy, and only the forgiven may be blessed. The Greek word for mercy, ἔλεος (eleos), is the outward manifestation of pity—God's attitude toward those who are in need. The Greek word for peace, εἰρήνη (eirene), is the contrast with strife, and it denotes the absence or end of strife. It is a state of health or well-being, and denotes a state of untroubled, undisturbed well-being. It is not a backward retreat but a forward victory.

The English word, **grace**, as defined in the Webster's II New College Dictionary, 2001, p.482, is:

"(ME divine love<OFr<Lat. gratia, good will<gratus, pleasing)
1. Apparently effortless charm or beauty of movement, form, or proportion. 2. A characteristic or quality pleasing for its charm or refinement. 3. A sense of fitness or propriety. 4. A disposition to be generous or helpful. 5. A favor rendered voluntarily. 6. Temporary immunity or exemption. 7. a. Divine love and protection bestowed freely on human beings. b. Protection or sanctification by the favor of God. c. An excellence or power granted by God. 8. A short prayer or blessing or thanksgiving said before or after a meal."

The Greek word for grace, χαρίς, is one of the most important words in the New Testament. It is built upon the root, χάρ, and there are about thirteen other words with this root, of which χαρά, or joy, is one. The total use of words with this root in the New Testament is 402.

One of these words is χαίρω, a verb meaning, "I rejoice, am glad, hail, greetings" (greeting form). It is used 74 times.

The word, χαρίζομαι, is used 23 times, and it means, "I give freely, grant, cancel, remit, forgive, pardon." From this word we get the word, charisma, which means: "1. Theol. a divinely gift of power. 2. the special influence or authority over large numbers of people." The word, "charismatic," is also from this word. Thus we are reminded of the charismatic movement of a few years ago, and even today we see some of the influences of that movement.

The word, εὐχαριστέω, is used 38 times, and it means, "I am thankful, give thanks, offer a prayer of thanks." From this word we get the word, Eucharist.

Χαρίς, or grace, is used 155 times, and it means, "grace, favor, gift, kindness." In the KJV it is translated "grace" 127 times. Other words that are used are, "favor, thanks, pleasure, liberality, benefit, joy, thankworthy, and acceptable."

Grace is also associated with many other words, such as, "graceful, graceless, disgrace, grateful, gratitude, ingratitude, congratulation." Over the years, I have had friends by the name of "Grace." It is a beautiful word. To many "men on the street" it is just a church word with no particular meaning to it. However, we who have had an encounter with the Almighty can sing with John Newton:

> *"Amazing grace! how sweet the sound, that saved a wretch like me! I once was lost, but now am found, was blind, but now I see.*
> *'Twas grace that taught my heart to fear, and grace my fears relieved; How precious did that grace appear the hour I first believed!*
> *Thro' many dangers, toils, and snares, I have already come; 'Tis grace hath bro't me safe thus far, and grace will lead me home."*

The song, Amazing Grace, was composed by John Newton, a man who, indeed, was a despised "wretch of a man." John was the son of a sea captain, and his mother died when he was the age of seven. Following his mother's death, he went to sea with his father. They had problems living together, so John left him and then fell into a sinful life of degradation—fighting, drinking, and jail.

At one point, John was a crewman on a slave ship, and he so infuriated the captain that he was made "a slave of the slaves." It took a destructive storm at sea, which almost took his life, for God to get his attention.

At the age of 39, John Newton became a minister, and during his fifteen-year pastorate at Olney, England, he composed Amazing Grace, along with several other hymns. Notice the time frame of the song: in verse 1, he tells about a time when he was "lost and blind"; in verse 2, he tells about the time he was saved by grace; and, in verse 3, he tells about grace carrying him through many troubling times. The last verse, which was written later by someone else, finished the time frame by shouting about grace being an eternal virtue:

"When we've been there ten thousand years, bright shining as the sun,
We've no less days to sing God's praise than when we first begun."

That song about God's "Amazing Grace" has blessed millions. Some years ago, the Christian Herald magazine polled its readers for their all-time favorite list of 50 hymns. Amazing Grace was ninth on that list. I have been singing it for eight decades, but it never gets old. Yes, God's grace is amazing! It can take a lost and blind sinner from the depths of a cesspool of iniquity and raise that person to the heights of eternal glory!

God's ultimate grace, Salvation, is not attained by works or barter; it is a free gift from the Almighty Ruler of the Universe! It is not for sale. There is no college or university that can dispense it. There are many degrees in a multitude of subjects that they can grant to their students, but not grace. No nation has the power to give it to its citizens. No doctor has the power to prescribe a pill for it.

Yet, this gift is more precious than the finest of elegant clothing; it is more precious than the most prestigious degree ever offered by any college or university in the world; it is worth more than "the cattle upon a thousand hills" and all the gold stored at Fort Knox.

This grace is a free gift to all who receive it in Christ Jesus our Lord. It is for the rich and the poor, the wise and the unwise, the educated and the uneducated, the black and the white, the old and the young, the slave and the free; it is to be received by faith. The word used for the way to salvation is also χαρίς. Our scripture text, Ephesians 2:1-10, tells us just how important Grace is:

> *"(1) You were dead in your transgressions and sins, (2) when you followed the evil ways of this present age, according to the ruler of the authority of the air, which is now operating in the sons of disobedience, (3) among whom we also conducted ourselves then <u>in the lusts of the flesh and the mind, and were by nature children of wrath, as the rest.</u> (4) <u>But God,</u> who is rich in mercy, because of the great love by which he loved us, (5) and when we were dead in trespasses, <u>made us alive in Christ Jesus—by grace you are saved—</u> (6) and raised us up and seated us in the heavenlies with Christ Jesus, (7) in order that in the coming ages he might show the exceeding riches of his grace in kindness toward us in Christ Jesus. (8) For you have been saved by grace through faith; and this is not from you, it is the gift of God— (9) not of works, lest anyone should boast. (10) <u>For we are</u>*

<u>his work of art</u>, created in Christ Jesus <u>for</u>
<u>good works</u>, which God had previously
prepared, that we should walk in them."

Salvation brings changes of lifestyle. We are saved by grace, but it is received through faith. We can be saved no other way. Good works can never be exchanged for it; money cannot buy it; there are no universities with the authority to impart it; but, it is available for everyone who is prepared to receive it. The sinner just needs to step up to the platform and receive it by faith. It brings salvation, and with salvation comes a new lifestyle. Old things have passed away; new things have arrived. It is adequate for every occasion.

Paul was given a thorn in the flesh. He begged the Lord 3 times for Him to take it away, but the Lord told him, "My grace is sufficient for you, for my power is perfected in weakness." He learned to look to God for power rather than to think about his weakness. Then he took pleasure in his weaknesses, in insults, hardships, persecutions, and difficulties, for the sake of Christ. In his weakness, the grace of God made him strong (2 Corinthians 12:7-10).

This is a lesson for us. We need to take what we have, in all our inadequacies, and commit our lives for His service. Then our bodies can become instruments for righteousness rather than instruments for wickedness. The same grace that was sufficient for Paul is still available for us. So, today, it is still sufficient for all who receive it in faith.

Salvation is available. Today is the day of salvation. Yesterday is gone, and tomorrow has not yet arrived. So, we only have today to receive this grace through faith. It is given to the "poor in Spirit," and it is available now. When we receive this grace, it means that we will have a new lifestyle. The works of the flesh have been exchanged for the fruit of the Spirit. The rebellious life has been exchanged for the surrendered life. It works through meekness. Wisdom tells us what we should do, and meekness gives us the integrity and stability to do it. The "now" time is with us. Now is the time to receive it! You can be relieved from the burden of sin. It can free you from depression, hatred, animosity, fornication, worry, drugs, and all the works of the flesh.

The new lifestyle is the fruit of the Spirit: love, joy, peace, long-suffering, kindness, goodness, faithfulness, meekness, and self-control (Galatians 5:22-23). This new lifestyle can be a help and a blessing to others. As you bless others, God will bless you with joy unspeakable.

Do you embrace it? Is this Amazing Grace a part of your life? If not, would you like to receive it? No one can force you to accept it. You cannot receive it by ritual. Baptism or the Lord's Supper does not have the efficacy to save. Good works are not the cause of Grace, but they are the effects of it. Grace brings joy to life and a new lifestyle. The wages of sin is death, but the grace, χάρισμα (charisma), of God is eternal life in Christ Jesus our Lord (Romans 6:23).

When Philip took the gospel to Samaria, and when they accepted it, "there was much joy (χαρά) in that city" (Acts 8:8). Paul wrote to the Ephesians to be kind to one another, tenderhearted, χαριζόμενοι (charizomenoi), forgiving one another as God in Christ, ἐχαρίσατο (echarisato), forgave them (Ephesians 4:32).

Woodrow Wilson told the story of being in a barbershop one day having his hair cut, when an unidentified man came in for a haircut and took the chair next to him. In a very short span of time, something had happened in the shop. Without being "preachy" at all, that man elevated the conversation in the shop to a new level, just by the way in which he talked to the man who was cutting his hair and to the others around him. In fact, Mr. Wilson said that he felt as if he had been in an evangelistic service. He said, without ever knowing his identity, that they had been touched by his personality and by the power of his presence. That man, as it turned out, was the noted and beloved evangelist, D.L. Moody, and he was simply being a "light" in a world of darkness!

Would you like to be the person who lights up the shop when he/she enters the room? With the help of Jesus, you can be that kind of a person. May we make the right decision and accept God's grace for our lives!

Compassion

One day when Jesus was in the temple court, the people gathered around him, and he taught them. The teachers of the law and the Pharisees brought a woman who had been caught in the act of adultery, and standing her in the midst, they said to him, "Teacher, this woman has been caught in the act of adultery. Now in the law Moses commanded us to stone such; therefore, what do you say?" (John 8:2-5). Evidently, they were not interested in catching the man who had been involved with the woman.

In response, Jesus stooped down and wrote on the ground with his finger. I have often wondered what he wrote. It must have been something significant, but we can only guess what it was.

As they continued questioning him, Jesus stood erect and said to them, "Let the sinless one of you cast the first stone."

Then Jesus stooped down and again began to write on the ground.

After listening to Jesus, they went away one by one, beginning with the oldest, until Jesus was left alone with the woman.

Then Jesus said to her, "Woman, where are they? Has no one condemned you?"

She said, "No one, Lord."

Then Jesus said to her, "Neither do I condemn you. Go, and sin no more."

The teachers of the law and the Pharisees were not interested in real righteousness. They thought that their trap for Jesus would cause him to say something negative about the law so they could condemn him. Their cold intellectual knowledge of the law had no compassion for the sinner.

Religion without compassion has no mercy for the sinner. But Jesus demonstrated that compassion for the sinner was from the heart of God.

Compassion is an exciting word of action. The word is a very important word. The Greeks had a noun and a verb that express this idea. The noun is σπλάγχνον (splanknon), and the verb is σπλαγχνίζομαι (splanknizomai). The noun is used 8 times in the New Testament, and in the KJV it is translated 6 times as "bowels," which is a Latin word, one time as "tender mercies," and one time as "inward affection." The verb is used 12 times, and each time the Latin word, "compassion," is used to translate the word into English. The literal meaning of the word is "bowels," or "intestines." Metaphorically, it is the expression of a very sensitive feeling. We might define it as a "gut feeling." The derivation of the word, "compassion," is: {ME compassioun<LL compassion<compati, to sympathize, ie. L com-, with + L pati, to suffer}. It is the sympathetic concern for the suffering of another, together with the inclination to give aid or support or to show mercy. Compassion is a noun, but the idea of "moved with compassion," gives it action.

Some people have compassion, but others do not. Compassion is love in action. Religion without compassion is dormant or dead. It is like a wagon without horses or a car without gasoline. The motor may be good, but if there is no fuel, the car will not go forward. The theologian may teach the word of God accurately, but if there is no compassion, his/her words will be without power.

Jesus was a man of compassion. When he was moved with compassion, he helped those who were in need. Matthew 9:36 and Mark 6 tells us about Jesus' ministry in Galilee. Jesus went about in all the cities and villages teaching in their synagogues, proclaiming about the kingdom of God and healing every disease and every illness. When Jesus saw the crowds, he had compassion for them, because they were distressed and helpless, like sheep without a shepherd. His compassion moved him to minister to them both in word and in action.

As Jesus went through Galilee, at one point a leper came to him begging him and keeling before him saying, "If you are willing, you can make me clean!" Jesus had compassion on him, and he stretched out his hand and touched him and said, "I am willing. Be clean." Immediately, the leprosy left him, and he was cleansed (Mark 1:39-42).

In Mark 6, it is recorded that after John had been beheaded, Jesus got into a boat and traveled toward a solitary place in the desert. When the people heard about it, they followed him on foot from the towns. When he got out of the boat, he saw a great crowd. Jesus then had compassion for them and healed their sick. When evening came, the disciples came to him and said, "This is a desert place and it is getting late. Dismiss them, so they can go to the farms and villages to buy for themselves something to eat." Jesus' response was, "They do not need to depart. You give them something to eat." With five loaves of bread and two fish, Jesus miraculously fed the multitude.

Later, as recorded in Matthew 15:32-39 and Mark 8:1-10, Jesus fed another multitude of 4,000 men. At that time, the crowds had been with Jesus for 3 days, and they had no food. He did not want to send them home without food unless they might faint on the way. Jesus had compassion for them, and he fed them with the 7 loaves and a few fish that were available to Him.

After the transfiguration (Mark 9:14-29), Jesus, Peter, James, and John came down from the mountain, and they met with the disciples and a large crowd of people. A man had brought his son, who was possessed by a spirit, to the disciples to be healed, but they could not heal him. Jesus asked the boy's father, "How long has he had this problem?" He said, "From childhood; and oftentimes it has thrown him into fire and into water to destroy him; but if you can, have compassion on us and help us!" Jesus replied, "You say, 'if you can!' All things are possible to him who believes." The father said, "I believe; help my unbelief!" and Jesus cast out the unclean spirit, and the boy was healed.

In Matthew 20:29-34, there is the account of a great crowd that followed Jesus as he left Jericho. There were two blind men sitting by the roadside. Hearing that Jesus was passing by, they cried out, "Lord, Son of David, have mercy on us!" Jesus stopped and called them to him and said, "What do want me to do for you?" They said to him, "Lord, that our eyes be opened." Jesus had compassion on them, and he touched their eyes; immediately they could see, and they followed him.

In his gospel, Luke uses the word, "compassion," 3 times. The first instance was when Jesus went to the city of Nain, when his disciples and a large crowd followed him. A man, who was the only son of a widow, had died and was being carried out. Jesus, seeing the mother, had compassion on her and said to her, "Do not weep." Jesus went to the coffin and touched it, and when the pallbearers stopped, he said, "Young man, I say to you get up." Then the young man sat up and began talking, and Jesus delivered him to his mother.

One time Peter came to Jesus and said, "How many times do I have to forgive my brother who sins against me?

Seven times?" Jesus said, "I do not tell you until seven times, but until seventy times seven."

In Matthew 18:23-35, Jesus told a parable of a king who wanted to settle accounts with his slaves. A debtor was brought to him who owed him ten thousand talents (which would have been millions of dollars in today's money). He could not pay, so his lord commanded that he, his wife and children, along with everything that he had, be sold and payment be made. The slave fell down before his master's feet, begging for mercy. His lord, filled with compassion, released him and forgave his debt. That slave then went out and found one of his fellow slaves who owed him a hundred denarii (perhaps less than 100 dollars), and seizing him by the throat said, "Pay me what you owe me!" The fellow slave fell down before him and cried out for mercy, but he refused and went and put him in prison until he could pay the debt.

When the other slaves knew what had happened, they were exceedingly grieved, and they went and told their lord what had happened. Then the lord said to the slave, "Wicked slave! I forgave you all that debt, because you entreated me; should you not have had mercy on your fellow slave as I had mercy on you." The lord was angry with him, and he delivered him to the tormentors until he could pay back his debt.

Why did Jesus tell that parable? He did not leave us in doubt. He said, "So also our Father in Heaven will do to you, unless you forgive your brother from your heart" (Matthew 18:35).

In another lesson on compassion (Luke 10:25-37), one day a lawyer stood up to test Jesus, and he asked a very profound question, "Teacher, what must I do to inherit eternal life?" Since he was a lawyer, Jesus responded by a question concerning the law saying, "What is written in the Law? How do you understand it?" He answered, "You shall love the Lord your God with all your heart, and with all your soul, and with all your strength, and with your entire mind, and your neighbor as yourself."

Jesus then said to him, "You have answered correctly. Do this and you will live." But he, wishing to justify himself, said to Jesus, "And who is my neighbor?"

Then Jesus told a story about a man going down from Jerusalem to Jericho. That road had a descent from about 2,500 feet above sea level near Jerusalem to about 800 feet below sea level at Jericho, and it ran through a rocky, desolate place, which provided places for robbers to hide. At one point, the man fell into the hands of robbers and was stripped and beaten and left half-dead on the side of the road.

A priest happened to come by, and seeing him, he went by on the other side of the road. Likewise, a Levite came by and also went by on the other side. Then a certain Samaritan traveler came by, and when he saw him, he had compassion upon him. He went to him and bound up his wounds, pouring on oil and wine, and putting him on his own animal, he brought him to an inn and cared for him. The Samaritan had compassion, and that made the difference between him and the priest and the Levite.

The dialog with the lawyer began with a theological question about eternal life, but it ended with a situation on a dangerous road between Jerusalem and Jericho. In a very subtle way, Jesus answered his question about eternal life. The person Jesus commended was neither the religious leader nor the lay associate, but he was a hated foreigner. The Jews viewed Samaritans as half-breeds. Samaritans and

Jews lived in hostility against one another, but Jesus asserted that love knows no boundaries.

Jesus ended by asking the lawyer a question, "Which of these three became neighbor to the one falling among the robbers?" The lawyer answered, "The one showing mercy to him," being careful not to mention that the man was a despised Samaritan. Jesus said, "Go and you do likewise."

A third lesson on compassion in Luke was the story about the prodigal son (Luke 15:11-32). Luke is the only gospel writer who records both the story about the good Samaritan and the story about the prodigal son in scripture. Jesus began his parable about the prodigal by telling about a man who had two sons. The younger son said to his father, "Father, give me my share of the estate." So, the father divided the property and gave him his share. The son then left the father's house with a pocketful of money. He was going to show the world how important he was. Truly, he went out to find himself. He went to a far county, and he was a hero to the worldy crowd, so long as he had money.

Needless to say, the son's money did not last. When his money was gone, so were his fair-weather friends. At one point, after losing all his money, he was hungry, so he got a job—not a good job, but the worst of all jobs—taking care of swine. He was so hungry that he wanted to eat what they were eating, but no one gave him anything. So there he was, next to the hogs that were wallowing in the mud. He was hungry, dirty, and with a low esteem for himself. He had gone out to find himself, and there he was, helpless and without hope. But then his thoughts turned to his father and the home he had left. He recalled that even the hired men had food to spare, but there he was starving to death. He thought to himself that if he went home, maybe his father would have mercy on him and let him be a hired hand.

So, heading home and while he was still a distance away, his father saw him and was moved with compassion. Running to him, he fell on his neck and fervently kissed him. The son said to his father, "Father, I have sinned against heaven and before you. I am no longer worthy to be called your son." But the father cut him off before he could finish his speech. He said to his hired hands, "Quickly! Bring out the best robe and put it around him, and put a signet ring on his hand and sandals on his feet. Bring and kill the fatted calf. Let us eat and celebrate. For this my son was dead and he is alive again; he was lost and has been found." And they began to celebrate.

Meanwhile, the older brother, who had been in the field, came near the house. He heard music and the celebration, and he called one of the lads to him and asked him what was happening. He said to him, "Your brother has come, and your father killed the fatted calf, because he is back and in good health." The older brother was angry, because he had no compassion, and he refused to go in. His father came out to plead with him, but he responded by saying to his father, "Lo, these many years I have served you and I have never disobeyed your orders, and you have never given me a goat to celebrate with my friends. But when this son of yours, who has squandered your property living with prostitutes, comes home, you killed for him the fatted calf!" The older brother would not acknowledge that he was his brother, but his father said, "...we had to celebrate and rejoice, because this brother of yours was dead but now he lives. He was lost but he was found."

To fully understand this 15th chapter of Luke, it is necessary to carefully read the first verse. The tax collectors and sinners were all coming to Jesus to hear him. But the Pharisees and scribes were grumbling among themselves saying, "This man receives sinners and eats with them." Eating with sinners was more than a simple association; eating with a person indicated acceptance and recognition.

Jesus responded with a lesson that contrasted the love of God with the exclusiveness of the Pharisees. He tells them about the lost sheep, the lost coin, and the lost boy. He was illustrating that heaven rejoices when the lost has been found. After he told them about the shepherd finding the lost sheep, he said, "I tell you, there will likewise be more joy in heaven over one repentant sinner than over ninety-nine righteous people who have no need of repentance." Similarly, after the woman had found her lost coin, she called together her friends and neighbors and said to them, "Rejoice with me because I found my silver coin that was lost." Jesus concluded by saying, "Likewise, I tell you, there is joy before the angels of God over one repentant sinner."

So, what have we learned from our study of compassion? We have seen many examples of Jesus having compassion. Jesus had compassion on the leper, so he touched him and the leprosy left him, and he was healed. When Jesus saw that the crowds which followed him were hungry and had no provision for bread, he had compassion for them, and taking 5 loaves and 2 fish, he fed the crowd of 5,000 men, not including women and children.

On another occasion, after seeing that a crowd that had been following him for 3 days had no food, Jesus had compassion on them, and taking 7 loaves and a few fish, he fed the crowd of 4,000 men, not including women and children.

Then, there was the time that Jesus had compassion on the demon-possessed boy and cast out the demon and healed the boy.

Also, Jesus had compassion for the blind men, so he touched their eyes and immediately they could see, and they followed him.

What does it mean for us to have the name of Christian? Does the "-ian" attached to Christ mean the diminutive of Christ? If so, that means that we are to have compassion and that we are anointed for service.

Dr. Luke

Luke and Paul were companions in the gospel ministry. Both of them, together, wrote more than half of the 136,872 Greek words of the New Testament. Luke wrote more words than did Paul. Luke wrote 37,897 words; Paul wrote 32,394 words. The total words for both of them was 70,291.

Paul was a theologian, so he needed authority for what he said and wrote. He let it be known that he had the authority from the Creator of heaven and earth. So, Paul tells the recipients of his letters and his teachings who he is and who he works for. He refers to himself as a slave, δοῦλος (doulos), of Jesus and that he had been commissioned to be an apostle, ἀπόστολος (apostolos), sent to the Gentiles. Paul's name is recorded in the New Testament 158 times. By comparison, Peter's name is mentioned 156 times and John's name is mentioned 135 times. Only Jesus is mentioned more than Paul, for some 917 times.

Luke was a historian, so he gathered facts concerning Jesus and wrote them in a scroll for everybody to read. If both of his books were in the same scroll, that would make the scroll about 54 feet long. That was too big to handle, so the theory is that if such a scroll existed at one time, it must have been cut into two pieces. A 27-foot scroll would have been much easier to handle than one 54 feet long. Regardless of the truth of this theory, Luke, the author of the Gospel of Luke and Acts, penned more words that any other writer of the New Testament. Never does Luke mention his own name in his work. His name is only mentioned 3 times in the entire New Testament, and on those times he was referred to by Paul.

It happened that Luke and Paul became lifelong friends. Their background and training were so much different. Paul was a Roman citizen, and he was born in Tarsus of Cilicia. As a young man, he was sent to Jerusalem to be taught at the feet of Gamaliel, who was one of the greatest teachers of that day. His father was a Pharisee, and Paul became a Pharisee of great authority, even becoming a member of the Jewish Sanhedrin. We know very little about Luke. He was a physician who was loved by his people. He was the only Gentile writer of the New Testament. Luke had prepared himself to be a physician; Paul had diligently studied the law to prepare himself for his lifework. It is interesting to see how the doctor and the lawyer met.

On his first missionary journey, Paul went with Barnabas to Galatia. During that time, Paul was stoned at Lystra and almost died, but they came back to Antioch with a great report about their journey. On the second missionary journey, Paul took Silas with him. They went through Galatia, and they wanted to go north to Bithynia, but the spirit of Jesus would not permit them to go. Instead, they traveled west to Troas, where they spent the night. During the night while at Troas, Paul had a vision. In his vision, Paul saw a man standing and pleading with him saying, "Come over into Macedonia and help us!" It was while they were preparing to travel to Macedonia that Luke appeared on the scene (Acts 16:10).

A very interesting question to ask is who was the man standing and pleading for Paul to come and help them. This is the first time that Luke was spoken of. Maybe, it was Luke that Paul saw in the vision, coming in person after the vision, because from that point Luke became a part of the missionary team. That was the beginning of the "we" passages, which included Luke as part of the group. Acts

16:10 says, "...*we* immediately sought to go forth into Macedonia, convinced that God had called *us* to evangelize them."

From Troas, the missionary team went on a straight course to Samothrace and spent the night there. The next day, they went to Neapolis, and from there they went to Philippi, which was a Roman colony and the most important city of Macedonia. Evidently, this was the city that was the place where the man seen in the vision was crying out for help. So, the team went on a beeline from Troas to Philippi, not stopping in the other cities to minister the gospel on the way. Philippi was the city of their destination.

On the Sabbath day, the missionary team went to a place of prayer, and they shared the gospel with some women who were there. Lydia, who was a dealer in purple goods from the city of Thyatira, was one of the women who were there. She received the gospel and became the first European to become a disciple of Jesus. It had been a man that Paul had seen in his vision, but it was a woman who became the first believer. Lydia and her household accepted the gospel of Jesus, and they were baptized and became members of the first church to be established in Europe.

The experience with the fortune-teller was the next challenge of the missionaries. This lady followed Paul and his companions for many days. She had a spirit of divination, and her practice of soothsaying had brought her masters a lot of money. She recognized that Paul and his companions were slaves of the highest God and that they were announcing the way of salvation. Paul was troubled that she had a spirit of divination, so he commanded, in the name of Jesus, for the evil spirit to come out of her. It did, and that ended her role as a fortune-teller. This made her masters so angry that they seized Paul and Silas and dragged them to the marketplace where the rulers were. They accused Paul and Silas of being troublemakers and of bringing in customs that were contrary to Roman law. So, the people rose up against them, and the magistrates ordered for their clothes to be torn off and for them to be flogged. After many lashes, they threw them into prison, and the jailer was charged to keep them securely. So, the jailer threw them into the inner prison and secured their feet in the stocks.

After the Lord rescued Paul and Silas from prison, they left Philippi, but Luke remained behind. It is an interesting conjecture that after the team traveled from Troas to Philippi, Luke may have stayed in Philippi to live, because there is no indication that he left Philippi. That may be one reason why the church in Philippi was so generous and compassionate. This new church had an exciting beginning, and both Lydia and her household, along with the Philippian jailer and his family, were the nucleus of the church. Luke may have been the sparkplug for this new church. We do not have the details of Luke's time in Philippi, but we do know of his involvement from the narrative of the New Testament. After leaving Luke in Philippi, four years later Paul picked up Luke in Philippi to take him on his trip to Jerusalem to deliver the special offering for the poor Christian church there.

Continuing on the second missionary journey, Paul and his companions left Philippi and went through Amphipolis and Apollonia to go to Thessalonica. For three Sabbath days, Paul was able to lecture in a local synagogue at Thessalonica. However, as sentiment began to turn against Paul, violence was not far away. The Jews had rallied the people, so the brethren sent Paul away under the cover of darkness to Berea. Trouble was there also, so the brethren sent Paul as far as Athens. Without the company of Silas and Timothy, Paul went to Athens, expecting them to join him as soon as possible. Paul spent some time in Athens, but later he went to Corinth, where Silas and Timothy did eventually join him. Paul went on to finish the second missionary journey, after staying more than two years in Corinth, then going to Ephesus and Caesarea and returning to Antioch.

After reporting his experiences to the church in Antioch, Paul went on his third missionary journey. He first traveled from place to place through the region of Galatia and Phrygia, strengthening the churches. Then Paul went through Ephesus, through Macedonia, and then back to Corinth. It was when he left Corinth to return to Jerusalem that he went back through Macedonia and stopped in Philippi to pick up Luke.

The Gentile churches in Macedonia and Greece had made up an offering for the poor Christians in Jerusalem. Paul was accompanied by Sopater, who was from Berea, Secundus from Thessalonica, Gais from Derbe, Timothy from Lystra, and Tychicus and Trophimus from the province of Asia. The men traveling with Paul went ahead to Troas and there waited for Paul and Luke.

Now that Luke had joined Paul in Philippi and they were on their way to Jerusalem, the "we" passages of Acts began again. In Acts 20:6, the scripture says, "...*we* sailed from Philippi after the Feast of the Unleavened Bread, and five days later joined the others at Troas where *we* stayed seven days."

When the missionary team returned to Jerusalem, the church received them warmly. Paul told them what God had done among the Gentiles through his ministry (Acts 21:19). Thousands of the Jews had believed, but they were zealous for the law.   Some had seen Trophimus the Ephesian in the city with Paul, and they assumed that Paul had brought him into the temple area.   As a result, the whole city was in an uproar, and the people came running in all directions.   They seized Paul and tried to kill him.   The commander of the Roman troops heard what was happening, so he took officers and soldiers and stopped the rioters from beating Paul to death.   To prevent Paul from being mobbed, he was taken to Caesarea, where he remained in prison for about two years.   Although Luke was with the missionary team when they came to Jerusalem (Acts 21:17), he did not go with Paul to Caesarea.

So, for the two years while Paul was in prison at Caesarea, we do not know what happened to Luke.   When Paul sails for Rome, that's when Luke re-enters the picture. In Acts 27:1, it says, "…it was decided that *we* would sail for Italy."   When they got to Rome, Luke was there with Paul, because Acts 28:16 says, "When *we* got to Rome, Paul was allowed to live by himself, with a soldier to guard him."

This was Paul's first imprisonment, which began, perhaps, in 59 A.D.   He was there for about 2 years, and he was released in 62 A.D.   While he was in prison, he wrote to Philemon, and he said that Luke was his fellow laborer. Also, when he wrote to the church in Colossians (4:14), Paul referred to Luke as "the beloved physician."

After Paul was released from his first Roman imprisonment in 62 A.D., he probably went to Spain.   After being free for five years, he was again put in prison in 67 A.D.   This time he was in the Mamertime dungeon.   It was there that he wrote his last letter to Timothy.   As his execution day was drawing near, many of his co-workers had deserted him.   He wrote in 2 Timothy 4:11 saying, "Only Luke is with me."

Praise God for men like Dr. Luke! If it had not been for Dr. Luke, we would not have known about the birth of Jesus at Bethlehem and the shepherds coming to see Jesus that night; we would not have known about the Good Samaritan; and, we would have never heard about the Prodigal Son.

We are indebted to Paul and Luke. Together, they gave us more than half of the New Testament. Their training as young men was very different; however, they worked side by side in their effort to give us the message of Jesus. Paul, the theologian, was eager to let his recipients know where his authority came from. His dynamic conversion was so life-changing that we are told about it three times in the book of Acts. Not only was he called to preach, he was commissioned to be an apostle. He let it be known that he was a slave of Jesus and that he was an Apostle sent to the Gentiles. Luke was a historian, and he had no interest in telling his recipients about who he was. His name is mentioned only three times, not by Luke himself, but by Paul (Colossians 4:14; Philemon 1:24; 2 Timothy 4:11). So, praise the Lord for Paul and Luke!

First Things First
(Matthew 6:24-34)

Jesus taught us that we need to put First Things First. In Matthew 6:24-34, Jesus tells us what things are the most important. He said:

"(24) No one can serve two masters. For he will hate the one and love the other or he will hold to the one and despise the other. You cannot serve God and mammon.

"(25) Therefore I tell you, do not be anxious for your life, what you shall eat or what you shall drink, or for your body, what you shall put on. Is not life more important than food and the body more than clothing? (26) Look at the birds of heaven; they do not sow or reap or gather into barns, yet your Father feeds them. Are you not more important than they? (27) Which of you by being anxious can add one minute to your life? (28) And why be anxious concerning clothing? Observe how the lilies of the field grow. They do not toil or spin. (29) But I tell you that Solomon in all his glory was not clothed as one of these. (30) But if God clothes the grass of the field, which is today and thrown into the oven tomorrow, will he not provide much more for you? O you of little faith! (31) Therefore do not be anxious saying, 'What shall we eat?' or 'What shall we drink?' or 'What shall we put on?' (32) For the

Gentiles seek after all these things, and your heavenly Father knows that you need all these things. (33) But first seek his kingdom and his righteousness, and all these things shall be added to you. (34) Therefore do not be anxious for tomorrow. Let tomorrow take care of itself. Each day has enough trouble of its own."

The kingdom must be sought after. It is not the road of least resistance; it is not drifting downstream with the current. It takes effort and determination to go upstream. It takes character and commitment to serve God. The carpenter builds the house after much preparation; the student receives the degree after much study. The seeker of the kingdom finds it after he/she surrenders his/her life to the King of all Kings.

Priorities must be established, and this is an everyday task for us. The businessman may have 10 letters on his desk waiting for his answer, but he must choose the one to start with. The farmer may have a dozen things to do, such as, tilling the soil, feeding the animals, planting the grain, etc. What shall be first? The schoolboy with lessons to prepare for the test must make decisions about whether to spend time on music or chemistry or math, or "shall it be a date with my girlfriend to go to the ball game?"

To have a good life, we must establish good priorities, and some are short-range while other are long-range. Jesus tells us about a rich farmer (Luke 12:16-21). His land produced abundantly, and he thought to himself, "What shall I do, because I have no place to store my grain?" His priority was to build bigger barns. After he had been successful in storing his grain, his priority was to relax and to enjoy the fruit of his labor. So, he said to himself, "Soul, you have laid up many goods for many years, relax, eat, drink, and be merry." The world would proclaim such a man as a very successful businessman, a man worthy and deserving to live out his sunset years in pleasure and ease. But God called him a fool, because he had worked hard to store up earthly treasures, but he had no heavenly treasures. Then, Jesus adds a word of warning to all of us: "So it is to those who lay up treasures for themselves but are not rich toward God." His problem was not that his barns were full, but that he had no treasures laid up in heaven.

Earthly blessings are insecure and are subject to moth and rust; thieves break in and steal earthly treasures; the national economy changes with the possibility of depressions, inflation, wars, and revolutions; earthly treasures are not transferable past this present life at the time of death. On the other hand, spiritual blessings are secure; moth and rust cannot touch them; thieves cannot break in and steal them; God's economy never changes; spiritual riches earn compound interest; and spiritual riches are transferable to our heavenly home at the end of life on earth, becoming eternal riches.

Each person has a different challenge in setting priorities. Youth is an excellent time to plan for the future by setting priorities. What will he/she do in preparation for his/her adult life? Shall it be to be a teacher? If so, one must spend years in preparation. The teacher must know the subject and how to teach it, because it is as hard to teach something you do not know as it is to come back from somewhere you have never been. If you are going to be a lawyer, you must spend years of preparation. If you are going to be a physician, you must prepare yourself to be eligible to get into medical school, and then you will have years of study and preparation before you begin your practice as a physician.

Most professions are honorable and good, but they can be used for evil as well as for good. But there are some professions that can only be used for evil. There are some people who are only interested in making money and indulging in the desires of the flesh. Some people are involved in selling and using illegal drugs; some are involved in promoting prostitution; some are involved in the promotion of wild parties and the consumption of alcohol; and some are addicted to pornography. Those involved in such activities are wicked and are on the road to hell and destruction.

So, what should be the first things in my life? This is a question that is relevant for us to consider today, now, because if we put the right things first, now, we can lay up treasures in heaven; and, each day can be a day of "love, joy, and peace!"

Decisions must be activated. What Master shall we serve, God or Mammon? Shall we live by sight or by faith? To serve one is to reject the other. Jesus has made the challenge: "But first seek his kingdom and his righteousness, and all these things shall be added to you. Therefore do not be anxious for tomorrow." The man waiting for the train, bus, or plane must be ready for the takeoff. Once he is aboard, whether or not he is ready, the decision has already been made.

To say that we trust in God and live a life of anxiety is a contradiction. It has the potential for setting up frustrations, causing emotional disturbances, and may lead to nervous breakdowns. To say that we love God but hate our neighbor is double-talk, for in 1 John 4:20, we read: "If anyone says, 'I love God,' but hates his brother, he is a liar.

For the one who does not love his brother, whom he has seen, cannot love God, whom he has not seen." And what about the person who is more concerned about the satisfaction of the desires of the flesh than the fruit of the Spirit? Jesus said, "If anyone wishes to come after me, let him deny himself and take up his cross and follow me...but whoever will lose his life for my sake and the gospel will save it" (Mark 8:34,35). To be a Christian means to be dead to sin but alive to God and His plan for us. Dependence upon God leads to happiness and serenity. "Blessed are the poor in spirit, for theirs is the reign of heaven" (Matthew 5:3).

How does this work out in everyday life? The person who has "a big mouth" and likes to gossip about his/her friends must surrender his/her tongue to the Lord so it can be used as an instrument of righteousness, rather than for evil. The person whose mouth is full of cursing and filthy talk must give up this cesspool of iniquity and replace it with proper words of encouragement. The salesman who lies about his product must learn to tell the truth. The fornicator must go to extreme means to overcome a life of sensuality, even as Jesus said: "But I say to you that everyone who looks upon a woman to lust for her has already committed adultery in his heart. So if your right eye causes you to stumble, pluck it out and throw it away, for it is better that one of the members of your body perish than that your whole body be thrown into hell" (Matthew 5:28-29).

Destinations will be reached. Daily we move toward our final destination. The farmer sows seeds in his fields. Some germinate more rapidly than others, but they are always of the same kind. Wheat produces wheat—not thistles! The law of the physical world is that we reap what we sow, and the law of the spiritual world is just as certain! "For whatever a man sows he will also reap...." (Galatians

6:7b). "The path of the righteous is like the first gleam of dawn, shining ever brighter till the full light of day" (Proverbs 4:18). Witness the drunkard, the adulterer, the thief, the dope addict, the slothful.

Louie Zamperini was a great athlete in his early days. When the Japanese war began, he went into the military and became a pilot. He had some scary experiences fighting the Japanese in the air, and on one mission he was sent in search of a missing bomber. Far out over the Pacific Ocean, engine failure sent their plane plunging into the ocean. Of the nine on board, only three survived the crash. And later, one of them died. The two left were on a raft for forty-six days, when they saw land. But before they reached land, a Japanese boat picked them up. For the next two and a quarter years, Louie was a captive of the Japanese military. He was tortured and abused in many ways.

When the war was over and he was back at home, he had nightmares of being tortured by one of the Japanese guards whom they called "the Bird." He married a beautiful lady, but that was not enough to get his life back together. He began drinking and fighting. His life was miserable. At one point, he decided to return to Japan and hunt down "the Bird" to strangle him. One night, he dreamed he was back in a death battle with "the Bird." A scream startled him awake. He was straddling his pregnant wife, hands clenched around her neck. He later abused their baby. So, Cynthia snatched the baby and left.

Cynthia tried to save the marriage. There was a tent meeting in Los Angeles with the Billy Graham Crusade. Cynthia went to the tent meetings and she became a believer. She then tried to get Louie to go to the meeting, but at first, he refused. Finally, he went, and he made a profession of faith, which changed his life. His hatred of "the Bird" turned into compassion. His marriage was saved and Louie became a witness for Jesus. That is what the Grace of God can do for anyone who surrenders to the God of compassion and grace.

What does it mean to put First Things First? If you have not received God's forgiveness, then that should be top priority for your life. Your life could be taken from you today, and as Jesus said, if we do not have treasures in heaven we are fools with no security (Luke 12:20-21).

As Romans 6:23 says, "...the wages of sin is death, but the gift of God is eternal life in Christ Jesus our Lord." To receive that gift, one must repent. In 2 Peter 3:9, it says, "...it is not his will for anyone to perish, but for all to come to repentance." Repentance means a change in lifestyle. Hatred is replaced with love; vengeance is replaced with mercy; grudges are replaced with forgiveness. To have treasures in heaven, one must get rid of the burden of sin, and the only way to remove sins is by the forgiveness of God.

In the Lord's Prayer, we ask God to forgive us our debts, as we have also forgiven our debtors (Matthew 6:12). Then, we are told: "For if you forgive others who trespass against you, your heavenly Father will also forgive you; but if you do not forgive others, neither will your Father forgive your trespasses" (Matthew 6:14-15).

How do we know when we have been forgiven? When God forgives us, He gives us a new life of compassion and love for others. He forgives us as we forgive others, so that means now we have compassion and love for the ones we have forgiven. It becomes a way of life, and we live in a state of compassion and love for others—our foes as well as our friends!

So, what shall we put first today? Our jobs, our health, our bank account, our education, and our status are all important, but nothing is as important as our bank account in heaven. Judgment day is coming, and may we be faithful and prepared for that awesome day to receive His welcome unto that eternal day!

Forgiveness

Man needs to be forgiven. The natural man is alienated from God; and, he lives in slavery to the works of the flesh. God loves him and wants to save him so that he can live in the blessedness of His grace.

McCartney said, "The greatest word in the Bible, the greatest word spoken in heaven or on earth, is the word, 'forgiveness.'"

The word, "forgive," comes from an Old English word, "forgiefan." The dictionary meanings for "*forgive*" are:

"1. To grant free pardon for remission of an offence, debt, etc.; to absolve. 2. To give up all claim on an account of; to remit (a debt, obligation, etc.). 3. To grant free pardon to (a person). 4. To cease to feel resentment against."

There are several Greek words that mean "to forgive." One such word, ἀπολύω (apoluo), is a verb that means "to set free, dismiss, relieve, to divorce, let go, pardon." It is translated as "divorce" in Matthew 5:31, where it says, "Whosoever shall **put away** his wife." In Luke 6:37, it is translated "forgiveness," where it says, "*forgive*, and you shall be *forgiven*." The word is used 66 times in the New Testament.

Another word, ἀφίημι (aphiemi), means "I let go, give up, divorce, cancel, forgive, leave, tolerate." It is used 143 times. It is found in Luke 9:60, where Jesus said, "**Let** the dead bury their dead." In Matthew 6:12, it is translated, "*forgive* us our debts, as we *forgive* our debtors."

Another word, ἄφεσις (aphesis), means "release, pardon, forgiveness." It is used 17 times. In Matthew 26:28, it is translated, "…for many are the **remission** of sins." In Ephesians 1:7, it is translated, "In him we have redemption through his blood, the **forgiveness** of our transgressions."

Finally, the word, χαρίζομαι (charizomai), means "I give freely, grant, cancel, forgive, pardon." It is used 23 times. In Luke 7:21, it is translated, "**he gave** sight to many of the blind." In Ephesians 4:32, it is translated, "be kind to one another, tenderhearted, **forgiving** one another as God in Christ forgave you."

The disciples asked Jesus to teach them how to pray. In Matthew 6:9-15, he responded by saying,

> " *'Our Father who is in heaven,*
> *hallowed be your name.*
> *(10) Your kingdom come,*
> *your will be done,*
> *on earth as it is in heaven.*
> *(11) Give us our daily bread.*
> *(12) And forgive us our debts,*
> *as we have also forgiven our debtors.*
> *(13) And lead us not into temptation,*
> *but rescue us from the evil one.'*

(14) For if you forgive others who trespass against you, your heavenly Father will also forgive you; (15) but if you do not forgive others, neither will your Father forgive your trespasses."

Man's greatest need is for God to forgive him. What does it mean to have God's forgiveness? It means that we have been set free. When Jesus began his ministry at Nazareth, he entered into the synagogue and stood up to read. It was from Isaiah that he read, and, as recorded in Luke 4:18-19, the scripture prophesied about the ministry of Jesus, saying,

"(18) The Spirit of the Lord is upon me, because he anointed me to evangelize the poor. He has sent me to proclaim liberty to the captives, and to give sight to the blind, to release the oppressed, (19) to proclaim the acceptable year of the Lord."

So, what is the meaning of God's forgiveness? One of its meanings is "to pardon." In Matthew 26:28, when Jesus instituted the Lord's Supper, he said, "...for it is my blood of the covenant being shed for many for the **forgiveness** of sin."

Another meaning of forgiveness is "to have deliverance." After Jesus read the scripture from Isaiah, he told the audience that the scripture had been fulfilled, because he was the one spoken of by the prophet. The word for forgiveness, ἄφεσις, is used twice in the Luke 4:18 scripture, once where it says, "to proclaim **liberty** to the captives," and also where it says, to "**release** the oppressed." God's forgiveness gives us freedom and releases us from oppression, thus making forgiveness also deliverance.

One other meaning for forgiveness is "to forget." In Hebrews 10:17, it says, "And their sins and iniquities will I **remember no more**."

So, when God forgives an individual, he cleanses his/her heart of all evil. He is saved by faith through grace to walk in the newness of life. That does not mean that there will not be consequences, because consequences always follow our works, whether good or evil, but, when we are forgiven, we can have sweet fellowship with the Eternal Creator. He loves us with a perfect love, and he has no grudges or ill will against us. The burden of sin is removed, so we can live in the sunshine of his grace. This personal relationship with Jesus gives us victory over the works of the flesh and fills us with the fruit of the Spirit, which Galatians 5:23 enumerates as, "love, joy, peace, long-suffering, kindness, goodness, faithfulness, meekness, and self-control."

In the Lord's Prayer, we are told how we can receive God's forgiveness. We are taught to pray, "And forgive us our debts, as we have also forgiven our debtors." Here "as" means "in like manner." We ask God to forgive us in the same way that we forgive those who may have sinned against us. Then, telling us what the consequences are if we do not forgive others, the scripture says, "For if you forgive others who trespass against you, your heavenly Father will also forgive you; but if you do not forgive others, neither will your Father forgive you."

When we have put ourselves in the spirit of receiving God's forgiveness, we will forgive all who may have done us wrong. We will no more have ill will or grudges, because they will be turned into thoughts of love and compassion. This love always accompanies God's forgiveness and his desire to bless us with his grace. So, in like manner, we have love and compassion for those who have wronged us.

True forgiveness means that we have no ill will, that the sins of the past are forgiven, and that now we want to help the ones we have forgiven. When God forgives us, fellowship is restored, and when we forgive others, fellowship is also restored. Just to say, "I forgive you," is not enough. A feeling of goodwill toward the perpetrator must also follow.

So, summed up in a nutshell, God's forgiveness means several things. In addition to our sins being blotted out, the joy of salvation floods our soul; a new life is given to us, because the old one has passed away; our birth to the new life gives us power to forgive others; and, we take on the nature of God, and holiness is established.

The Bible gives us many examples of true repentance. One such example is found in Joseph, the son of Jacob, who was treated harshly by his brothers. When Joseph searched out his brothers at the request of his father, his brothers used the opportunity to vent their jealousy of him by attacking him, with the intent to destroy him. They first put him in a well, and later they sold him as a slave to some traders who were going to Egypt. In an attempt to cover their crime, they killed a beast, putting the blood on Joseph's robe, and they convinced Jacob, their father, that Joseph had been killed by a wild animal.

Years later, Joseph became prime minister in Egypt, being second only to the Pharaoh. When there was a famine in the land, Jacob sent his sons to Egypt to get grain. Though his brothers did not recognize him, the very person from whom they were forced to petition to buy grain was their brother, whom they had treated so badly. When the time came that Joseph revealed his identity, his brothers fell on their knees and begged for mercy, realizing that Joseph then had the power to destroy them. Although Joseph could have gotten revenge, he did not do so, because he was a man who loved those who had tried to destroy him. He said, "Fear not: for am I in the place of God? But as for you, ye thought evil against me; but God meant it unto good, to bring to pass, as it is this day, to save much people alive. Now therefore fear ye not: I will nourish you, and your little ones" (Genesis 50:19-21). He then comforted them and spoke kindly to them. Joseph had his opportunity to make his brothers pay for their mistreatment of him. But Joseph forgave them and blessed them with his kind treatment of them.

Then, there is the example of Stephen, a man who forgave the ones who stoned him to death. As he was dying, he said, "Lord, do not hold this sin against them." Then he fell asleep. Even though he was murdered, his last concern was for the ones who stoned him.

A different kind of example is found in the book of Esther, in the story of a man who did not forgive. This man's name was Haman, and he was the powerful, right-hand man to King Xerxes. The book of Esther records that "All the royal officials at the king's gate knelt down and paid honor to Haman, for the king had commanded this concerning him," giving Haman special honor by the subjects of the kingdom. However, there was one Jew by the name of Mordecai "who would not kneel down or pay him honor." This made Haman very angry. When he learned that Mordecai was a Jew, it was not enough just to vent his displeasure on one man, but he sought to kill all the Jews in the kingdom. In addition, he built a seventy-five feet high gallows for the purpose of hanging Mordecai. However, before he could carry out his evil plan, Esther made a banquet for the king and Haman. She pleaded for the deliverance of her people, the Jews. When the king learned that it was Haman who was behind this evil thing, he had Haman hanged on the gallows that he had made for Mordecai. What a tragedy. Ill will always leads to bad things.

Another tragic story is the account of Herodias, who had a grudge against John the Baptist. John had been saying to Herod that "It is not lawful for you to have your brother's wife." Herodias "was filled with hatred and wanted to kill John the Baptist but she could not." However, an opportunity came on Herod's birthday when Herod gave a banquet for his high officials, his military commanders, and the leading men of Galilee. The daughter of Herodias danced before the king and so pleased him that he promised her with an oath, "Whatever you want I will give you, up to half my kingdom." She asked her mother, Herodias, what she should ask for, and she said, "the head of John the Baptist on a platter." The evil deed was done. What awful advice for a mother to give to her daughter. She was offered half of the kingdom, but she settled for the head of a godly man who told her the truth. We can see what awful things can happen when people follow the works of the flesh!

It is always good to live in the shadow of God's forgiveness; and, it always results in devastation to live in unforgiving hostility against God. We have a perfect example of this in the record of Cain and Abel, found in Genesis 4:1-12. Cain was the firstborn of Eve, but she later gave birth to another son, Abel. Cain became a farmer, but his brother, Abel, kept flocks. At one point, Cain brought an offering to the Lord of the first fruits of the soil, while Abel brought the fat portions from some of the firstborn of his flock. The Lord looked with favor on Abel and his offering, but he did not look with favor on Cain and his offering. As a result, Cain became very angry, and his face was downcast. Then the Lord said to Cain, "Why are you angry? Why is your face downcast? If you do what is right, will you not be accepted? But if you do not do what is right, sin in crouching at your door; it desires to have you, but you must master it."

Sin is like a wild beast ready to pounce on its victim. Sin, in the form of depression, can cause a person to kill himself/herself, whereas passion can cause a person to commit adultery; and, anger can cause a person to murder another person. Cain's problem was anger. It was first anger against the Lord, but it festered and was later directed against Abel, his brother. The Lord told him that he must master it, but his plea was not heard.

Eventually, Cain lured his brother into the field. While they were there, Cain attacked his brother, Abel, and killed him. The Lord told Cain, "Your brother's blood cries out to me from the ground. Now you are under a curse and driven from the ground, which opened its mouth to receive your brother's blood from your hand."

Whatever our besetting sin is, we need to be forgiven by the Almighty. It needs to be done, and we have the secret for achieving it. If we can forgive others who trespass against us, then God is delighted to forgive us our trespasses. God is holy, so he cannot forgive those who are filled with hostility, the works of the flesh, or a depraved mind. We must surrender to him our sinful nature so we can receive his wonderful grace. Then, we can live in the sunshine of his glory.

Good For Evil

Jesus invited everyone to follow him but they had to commit themselves to his leadership. He said to everyone, "If anyone wishes to come after me, let him deny himself and take up his cross daily, and follow me. For whoever wishes to save his life will lose it, but whoever loses his life for my sake will save it. For what does it profit a man it he gains the whole world and loses his own soul or destroys himself?" (Luke 9:23-25).

On another occasion Jesus told his followers what they must do to be a part of his kingdom. Great crowds accompanied him; and Jesus turned to them and said, "If anyone comes to me and does not hate his father, mother, wife, children, brothers, sisters, and even his own life, he cannot be my disciple. Whoever does not bear his cross and follow me cannot be my disciple" (Luke 14:25-27).

In Luke 14:26, the Greek word for hate is μισέω. It means to hate, regard with ill-will; to detest, abhor; its usage in the N.T. also means to regard with less affection, love less, esteem less. In Romans 9:13 another form of this word is used and it tells us, "Jacob I loved, but Esau I hated." He was saying that he chose Jacob to be the father of his chosen people, even though Esau was the firstborn. This passage of Scripture only means that HE chose Jacob instead of Esau. God loves all his creation.

In our Scripture passage in Luke 9:23 (also found in Matthew 16:24), we are told that to be his disciple, we must put him first, even above our family or any other relationships, and that we must take up the cross and be ready to meet all extremes. The Greek word for cross here is σταυρός, which means a stake, a cross; the punishment of the cross; to take up, or to bear one's cross, to be ready to encounter any extremity.

The Bible also tells us that we are never to return evil for good, or evil for evil, but always to return good for good, or good for evil. In Romans 12:17-21, we are admonished to live in peace with everyone, and we are told never to take revenge, because that is the prerogative of God. It says in Deuteronomy 32:35, and repeats in Romans 12:19, "Vengeance is mine, I will repay," says the Lord.

Jesus tells us how to live. In Luke 6:27-36, He tells us to love our enemies (1), to do good to those who hate us (2), bless those who curse us (3), and to pray for those insulting us (4). Going further, Jesus said, "To the one striking you on the cheek, turn to him the other also, and from the one taking your coat, do not prevent him from taking your shirt (5). Give to the ones asking you (6), and from those who take your things, do not demand that they bring them back (7). Treat others as you would like for them to treat you (8)."

In these words of Jesus about dealing with good and evil, there are eight imperatives. The first one is to love our enemies. Let us examine each of these imperatives of Jesus, separately. The Greeks have 4 words for love. Two of them were the ones used in the New Testament repeatedly. They are the ones we will examine.

One of these Greek words is ἀγαπάω, which means to love, value, esteem, feel or manifest generous concern for. This word is the verb. The companion noun is the word ἀγάπη, ης, ἡ, which means love, generosity, kindly concern, devotedness, esteem.

The other Greek word is φιλέω, and it means to love, to manifest some act or token of kindness of affection; to kiss. This is the verb. The adjective form (nom. sg. m.) of the word is φιλός, which means loved, dear; as a subst., a friend; a congenial associate. Another form of the word, φίλη, means a female friend.

1. Love Your Enemies.

So we are to love (esteem) our enemies. Most people think that it is good to love our neighbors, but to hate our enemies, but Jesus had a better way. He said that we are to love our enemies. This word is ἀγαπάω which means to esteem.

Most of the time the word is used in a good sense, but sometimes it is used in a bad sense, because we do not always esteem the good things.

Let us look in John 3 and compare how this word, esteem, is used. In John 3:16, it says, "For God so loved the world, that he gave his only begotten Son that everyone believing in him may not perish but may have eternal life." But in John 3:19, the scripture says, "This is the condemnation, that the light has come into the world and men loved darkness rather than the light, for their deeds were evil. The same word (esteem) is used for love.

Looking also in 1 John 2:15, it says, "Do no love the world or the things in the world. If anyone loves the world, the love of the father is not in him." The words for love are all the same.

I think that the best English word to describe this Greek word is esteem.

In this first imperative we are examining, Jesus tells us to love (esteem) our enemies. We may ask ourselves the question, "Why should we love our enemies?"

Jesus gave us the Great Commission in Matthew 27:19, "Therefore as you go, make disciples of all nations." We must love people if we are going to make disciples of them. So we send missionaries to the foreign countries of the world. However, we are living in a day when millions of foreign people have come to our land, so we have a great opportunity to minister to them right here.

Muslim immigrants are claiming the U. S. as theirs. Hundreds of golden-domed mosques and Islamic centers are going up across our nation. An estimated 250,000 Middle Easterners are immigrating to the U. S. each year.

There is an organization called Christ for All Peoples. And they go to the mosques and other places where Muslims are and give them Christian materials, included a DVD of JESUS. They report that almost 100 percent gladly accept them. They also report that tens of thousands have come to Christ and hundreds of house churches and Christian fellowships have been established in predominantly Muslim neighborhoods; and, many have become part of local churches.

Right here, in Bryan/College Station, Texas, we have a unique opportunity of meeting peoples from the nations of the world, because we are near A&M University, where there are students from many foreign countries.

The mission field is here. Dr. Curtis Lard, a dean of A&M University for 20 years, tells us that there are students in the university from 130 foreign nations. What a challenge we have to establish a friendship with the peoples of the world. Whether friend or foe, let us love them and tell them about Jesus.

2.   *Do Good To Those Who Hate Us.*

After we have learned to love (esteem), our next imperative is to <u>do good to those who hate us</u>, which is a great challenge. Yes, it is a great challenge for us all, but it is a great opportunity for us. For loving our enemies, who hate us, gives us spiritual growth. A heart of practicing love helps us grow in the grace of God, and doing good to those who hate us gives us more spiritual growth. If we do that, we have returned good for evil. But, if we respond to hate, evil for evil, we have sinned and fallen short of the glory of God. Hate and the resentful heart is a hindrance to all spiritual growth.

Remember what Paul wrote to the Romans (12:21), "Do not be conquered with evil, but conquer evil with good." He gave us the method of responding to evil. So we cannot reject our enemies who hate us, but we must respond with something good. We must always remember that some people may hate us, but that does not give us reason to hate them. If we do them good, they may even decide to love us. However, if they are not changed in their hatred for us, we are still blessed because we have been faithful to our heavenly calling. Doing good gives us sweet memories to bless us; but doing evil leaves us with nightmares to cope with.

3.   *Bless Those Who Curse You.*

Then our third imperative is for us to bless the ones cursing us. Here general kindness is shown to those who are attempting to bring evil upon us. If we are living in the flesh, we will respond by more cursing upon the perpetrator. But if we are slaves of Jesus, he will teach us the way of the godly life, and cursing is not the way of the godly life. We are always compelled to respond to evil by good, and we know that cursing is not good, so we must respond some way that would be good. In the flesh, we cannot, but in the spirit, we can, such as some word of encouragement or some act of kindness. It may not change your opponent, but it will be a means of cutting off any future cursing of your opponent.

4.   *Pray For The Ones Insulting You.*

The fourth imperative of our study is found in Luke 6:28, which says, "…and pray for the ones insulting you." There are times when there is no opportunity or need to encounter those who abuse us. So we are admonished to pray for them. The flesh would cry out to God to condemn them, but we are told that vengeance belongs to God. So we do not need to get even with our abuser. We all must pay for our sins, but it is not our job to punish those who harass us. I am commissioned to return good for evil. I must leave that in the hands of the Almighty. He knows how to do it, but if I start doing bad things to get even, that would be trying to conquer evil by evil. As a slave of Jesus, I must obey him and overcome evil with good. Therefore in my prayers I must pray earnestly that the abuser will repent of his/her unholy ways and find a new life style that will give him/her a blessed and useful life.

5. *Turn The Cheek To The One Striking You.*

Remember that in our fifth imperative in Luke 6:29 that "To the one striking you on the cheek turn to him the other also; and the one taking your coat, do not prevent him from taking your shirt."

The Greek word for "striking" is τύπτω, a present participle. It means to beat, hit, strike, wound, injure. It was a violent blow with the fist rather than a contemptuous slap on the cheek, and the participle would suggest that it is linear (repeated) action. So if you doubled up your fist and went after him in like manner it would end up in a bloody, dirty fist fight.

Fist fighting is an attempt to solve the problem by the works of the flesh, but a better way is solving the problem by the spirit, and that is to return good for evil. And if the opponent takes the outer garment, do not prevent him from taking the inner garment. So we are admonished not to confront our oppressor in the flesh. In making this response, Good for Evil, I will be blessed of the Lord.

Once when I was a boy, I went with my family to Jacksboro, Texas, to some special event. It may have been a rodeo, or a carnival, or some school tournament, but that I cannot remember. I only remember one thing about that day. Two men had a bloody fist fight. It was an awful sight to see and I still remember it after about 85 years. That was evil then and fist fights are evil now. And we, as disciples of Jesus, are not to respond to evil with evil. The response must always be good for evil even though we may be mistreated.

6.   *Give to everyone asking you.*

In this approach to doing good, our sixth imperative in Luke 6:30 says, "Give to the ones asking." That is right, we are told to give to everyone asking of us. However, we are not told to give what they ask us to give. We must never reject anyone, but we must be good stewards of our wealth, and we must be thinking how the money would be used. If we give the money to the drug addict, it may be used to buy illegal drugs. If we give money to the bum who is too lazy to work, we may be contributing to a lifestyle of irresponsibility. If we are prayerful, we usually understand what we should do.

Money may not be the answer. It may be a matter of advice or encouragement. After all, we are called to be evangelists rather than bankers. And our money may be limited but the grace of God is available and much more powerful. Money may be a quick fix, but grace is an eternal fix. If we prayerfully seek the Lord about what we ought to do and do his will, we both can be blessed in this transaction.

7.   From Those Taking Your Things Do Not Demand Them Back.

In examining our seventh imperative, we realize that the perpetrator who took your things will not want to bring them back. The encounter would cause more problems. So we are taught that it is better to suffer loss than to demand retribution to the one who has wronged us. And this personal loss can give us opportunities to return good for evil. And this personal encounter may give us a way to lay up some treasures in heaven.

8.   As You Wish Others to do to You, Do to Them Likewise.

Our eighth, and last imperative, in Luke 6:31 tells us, "And as you wish that men may do to you, do you likewise to them." In Matthew 7:12 we have the same teaching: "Therefore treat others the way you would like to be treated; for this is the law and the prophets." This teaching is commonly called The Golden Rule. We are not told to treat others the way they treat us, but the way we wish they would treat us. These commands (imperatives) are not easy to follow, but they are from the Holy Bible, and living by them we grow in the grace and knowledge of our Savior.

Jesus said if you want to be my disciple you must take up your cross and follow me, and his lifestyle is not of the flesh but of the spirit of love and compassion. In Luke 6:32-36 he tells us that our lifestyle must be more than the lifestyle of the world.

If you only love those who love you, what credit is that to you? The sinners love the ones loving them.

If you do good to the ones doing good to you, what credit is that to you? Even sinners do the same as you.

And if you lend to whom you expect to receive back, what credit is that to you? Even sinners lend to sinners that they may receive back the equal things.

You are to love your enemies, do good, and lend to them without expecting anything back; and your reward will be great and you will be sons of the most high, because He is kind to the unthankful and sinners. Be compassionate as your Father is compassionate.

Some Scriptures are not expected to be taken literally. Witness Matthew 5:29. So if your right eye causes you to stumble, pluck it out and throw it away for it is better that one of the members of your body perish than that your whole body be thrown into hell. (30) And if your right hand causes you to stumble, cut it off and throw it away …

It is obvious that this does not refer to the fleshly body, because the body only does what the mind tells it. It is a great teaching; but, it is not found in the literal interpretation of it.

In Revelation 12:4, we are told that the dragon with a sweep of his tail cast a third of the stars to the earth. We know that the stars are bigger than the earth. So there is no way that the earth is big enough for that many stars.

In Matthew 7:5, we are told: Hypocrite! First take the log out of your eye, and then you will see clearly to take the splinter out of your brother's eye.

So there are places in the Bible that we are not supposed to take literally, but I think this passage of Scripture in Luke is not one of them. We may not be mature enough to do this, but I think this is the big thing to do!

And if we practice it we will be blessed and we will be better prepared for our next challenge that comes our way.

So, in conclusion:

1. ***Love your enemies***. After the resurrection of Jesus, and before his ascension he commissioned his disciples, "As you go, make disciples of all nations." And if we are going to make disciples of all nations we must love them; therefore, we must love them.

2. ***Do good to those who hate you***. If people hate you, that is no reason for you to hate them. We are to return good for evil and this is a challenge for us, maybe by a kind word of encouragement or a benevolent deed of kindness.

3. ***Bless those who curse you***. God sends sunshine and rain to those who curse him, and we who live by his grace must do likewise; and remember, we are to overcome evil with good.

4. ***Pray for those who mistreat you***. We must forgive those who trespass against us. If we do not, then we will not be forgiven of our sins. Jesus said, "For if you forgive others who trespass against you, your heavenly Father will also forgive you; but if you do not forgive others, neither will your Father forgive your trespasses" (Matthew 6: 14, 15).

5. ***Refuse to continue a fist fight***. To continue a fist fight would be returning evil for evil, and we are never to do that. It would be better to suffer for evil than for us to return evil for evil. We must overcome evil with good.

6. *Give to him who asks you.* We are never to reject anyone, but it does not mean that we will give what we are asked for. They may want money, but they may need a word of encouragement more. Money is an immediate fix, but grace is an eternal one. Our calling is to be evangelists, not bankers.

7. *To the one taking your things do not demand them back.* To encounter someone who stole your things would very likely cause conflict, sometimes even violence. So it is better to suffer loss than to contest a violent person.

8. *Treat others as you would like for them to treat you.* This should be easy for us to do. We are only asked to treat others as we would want to be treated.

So this is our job. We who live by the grace of the Almighty have the resources to accomplish this lifestyle. And when we do, we are sharing the gospel with the multitudes. This is our calling; let us hasten to accomplish it!

Good News

Today, I want to tell you about some Good News! It is the best news that I have ever heard. I get a newspaper everyday, The Eagle, but the news in the daily newspaper is often more bad than good. The front page of The Eagle for 1 July 2009 reported, "Iraq blast kills 33 after U.S. exit; Faculty Senate votes against chancellor; Quintero in jeopardy of losing his property; and A&M professor Conant dead at 54."

Although there is much bad news everyday, I want to tell you about some Good News today that is Good News everyday. In fact, that has been a big part of my job for many years, but before I tell you about my vocation, let me tell you about how I got that assignment.

As a kid growing up on a small farm, I used to think a lot about God. I kind of pictured Him as someone about like my Grandpa Wilton. After getting more learning, things got bigger and more complicated. When the columnist, George Will, addressed the graduation class at Miami University, he gave some interesting speculations about our universe. He said, "the sun around which earth rotates is one of perhaps 300 billion stars in the Milky Way, which is a piddling galaxy next door to nothing much. There are perhaps 40 billion galaxies in the still-unfolding universe. If all the stars in the universe were only the size of the head of a pin, they would fill Miami's Orange Bowl to overflowing more that 3 billion times."

I do not know the accuracy of those statistics, but I do know that we have an awesome universe, and we believe that the one who created it still controls it. We also believe that Jesus the Messiah was His Son, sent to the little place called "earth" to redeem us. He still lives among His people, called the church. All the members in His "body" have a part in reconciling the world to Christ. We are His ambassadors sent on a mission.

When I was a boy, we had protracted meetings (later called revivals) for about 2 weeks each summer. It was during one of those meetings that I accepted Jesus as my Savior. It was a great experience, and at the end of the revival, Herbert Parrish, Kenneth Hannah, and I were baptized in a big tank of water in one of the local pasturelands, where the cattle came to drink. At that time, I was about 13 years old.

Sometime later, I became involved with the exciting experience of college life. I then had so many things to do that I began to neglect the spiritual side of life. By then, I really did not think that is was necessary to go to church, or to pray, or to follow those old-fashioned ways of Pa & Ma, thinking they were outdated! I was really having a ball, and I was questioning those values taught to me earlier, asking myself, "What is so bad about gambling? How could a little game of poker be bad for anyone? Drinking a few beers and some whisky might be good for me? And, what is wrong with ballroom dancing? It just might make me become a more prestigious person?" I didn't know it then, but I was getting ready for some life-changing behavior!

Then, all of a sudden, the world changed for me. God gave me some other questions to ponder, along with some answers without questions. I began to ask, "What is life for, anyway?" I remember seeing students rushing in every direction for classes, and the idea of death met with me that day as I was planning my life for the future! It became very real to me that we are all going to die and that life is meaningless without something eternal to live for. For two or three weeks I was in a stupor. I then asked myself, "Where is God?; Is there anything of an eternal nature that I can hold on to?" For awhile, life was miserable, and I had no hope in all that worldly living. It seemed that I was in a deep pit calling out for help. I could see that life, real life, was not found in education, money, popularity, status, or any other thing that this world could offer.

Then, the light began to dawn. I realized that God is in the universe, that He is here among His people, that He loves His people, and that He is not willing that anyone of His creation would perish. But, He is holy, and if we are going to live in His presence, we must be holy! His ways are so much better than my ways. Holiness is so much better than worldliness, just as light is better than darkness. His will is so much better than my will. In my personal struggle, I surrendered my life for His service. That is when God gave me the job of telling others about the Good News!

The Gospel of Christ is the Good News. The word, Gospel, comes from the middle to old English word, "godspel," which was a combination of god, or good, with spell, or tidings, and its meaning is "good tidings," or "good news." The Gospel is indeed Good News. The Greek form of the word is εὐαγγέλιον (euaggelion). It is actually from two Greek words, which are εὐ (eu), an adverb meaning "well," and ἄγγελος (aggelos), meaning "messenger," or "angel." Εὐαγγέλιον (euaggelion) is used 76 times in the New Testament, being translated as "Good News."

After the Lord touched me, the questions were no longer for me whether to gamble, play poker, go dancing, or to drink intoxicating liquors. The question I then asked myself was, "How can I use my life to carry out the work that the Almighty created me for?" Those, supposedly, old-fashioned ways of my parents then became a foundation for me to begin the ministry of telling others about the Good News. A book of God's word, the Bible, was given to me, and, as then, it tells us about the Good News.

Using the Good News of God's word, my first message was from Romans 1:14-16. The title of my first sermon was, "I am not ashamed of the Gospel!" This message that I am not ashamed of is a message for everyone, whether wise or unwise, Jew or Greek, black or white, young or old, rich or poor. Over the years, my Master has sent me to preach this wonderful message to many peoples and places of different cultures, which include India, Japan, and South America. This message of salvation is not in government schools of higher learning. In this message is proclaimed eternal verities that everyone must sooner or later struggle with.

I am not ashamed of Jesus, the Christ (Messiah) of the Gospel. Jesus is my hero! He came from a poor family, even being born in a manger. But, that is of no importance. He is still my Hero! He was crucified as a criminal, dying on a cruel cross for the sins of the world. He is my hero! He arose from the grave to lead his church, and his last words were that he would return someday. He is my hero! No, I am not ashamed of Jesus.

I am not ashamed of the Life of the Gospel. It is a new lifestyle. It is a life of repentance, making it possible to be a part of the kingdom of Heaven. The works of the flesh have been traded for the fruit of the Spirit. It is a life of Christian commitment. The cross is central in the message of God's kingdom. We must be Holy, because He is Holy, and without holiness, we will never be a part of His kingdom. In this new life, we receive an imputed righteousness. The Holy Spirit was given to us, and it is through the leading of that Spirit that we can do His will.

We live by faith, not by sight. By His grace, we can be on top of circumstances.

What really is this Good Message? It is not telling us that we are sinners, because we already know about that. The Good News is that even though we are sinners, there is a way out! Even though we have fallen into the cesspool of sin, there is hope. Jesus died for the sinner, and sins can be wiped out. As a result, the filthy can become clean; the mean can become good; and, the profane can become holy. Isn't that a beautiful message? We, who have accepted Jesus, are called to share this precious message of salvation.

Is the Good News really good? What does it mean to a person whose life has become a nightmare because of the burden of sin? It means that Jesus came to be an offering for our sins and that we can come to him and have our sins forgiven. The shame and embarrassment can be taken away. We can submit ourselves to God and resist the devil, and he will flee from us. When we draw nigh to Him, He draws nigh to us. When we surrender to Him, we can cleanse our hands, and He will cleanse our hearts. This is the best news that the sinner ever heard!

What does it mean to the person whose world has caved in? Whether one is suffering from sickness, such as knowledge of a deadly cancer, or poverty due to the loss of all worldly goods, or grief from the death of a loved one, there is hope.

For the dying man, is there a way out? Yes, there is. Paul said in Romans 8:28, "We know that all things work together for good to those loving God, who are called according to his purpose." That does not mean that everything that happens is God's will. But, it does mean that there is a way out of all circumstances. His grace is sufficient. The person who is facing death must focus on the true meaning of life. Earthly life in temporal. That is the way God made it, so it must be good. It is a call for us to minimize the physical and temporal and to maximize the spiritual and eternal. Then we can redeem the precious time that is left, by focusing our minds on god's grace.

For the person who has lost everything and has no clothes to wear, no place to live, and nothing to eat or drink, is there a way out? Jesus said, "I tell you, be not anxious for your life, what you shall eat or what you shall drink, nor for your body, what you shall put on. Is not life more than food and the body more than clothing? Look at the birds of heaven, they do not sow nor reap or gather into barns, yet your heavenly Father feeds them. Are you not more important than they?" Then we have the promise, "But first seek His kingdom and His righteousness and all these things will be added to you" (Matthew 6:25-33).

For the person who has been devastated because of the loss of a loved one, is there Good News? Yes, there is comfort from the God of grace. God is to be worshipped. If we put anyone before Him, we have fallen into idolatry. God is sufficient. We have relatives, friends, and associates, but none are as important as our God. If He is with us, we are not alone. We cannot live in the past. We must always live in the present, and while we are here, there is something constructive that we can do. Self-pity is not good, but while we are here, we can live for Jesus and for others, which will give us purpose in life. Paul wrote, "...while we do not fix our gaze upon the things which are seen, but upon the things which are unseen, for the things which are seen are temporal, but the things which are not seen are eternal" (2 Corinthians 4:18).

For the person who is disappointed and lonely, is there any Good News? I think so. It may be that a marriage has gone sour, or it may be that a friendship has gone cold. It may be that the children have gone astray. Many things can become problems in our lives. What we need to do is to refocus our lives. Some things we can change, but other we cannot. Suppose we lose our job. That might mean that we must lower our standard of living. Our status may be changed and our "importance" may be diminished, but we need to ask ourselves, "What is really important?"

So, look at today as a gift from God. We can choose the good and reject the evil, or, we can choose the evil and reject the good. But, the consequences will not be the same. The Good News is that we can choose the good, and good things will follow.

The good News is that our sins can be forgiven. Even though we have sinned and filled our lives with evil, we can turn to God, and He will forgive us and place our feet on solid ground. Then, life can be a blessing to us and to others.

The Good News to the person who is at the door of death is that there is hope for the few days left and for all eternity.

The Good News to the bereaved is that life still goes on and that only God is to be worshipped. While we have life, there is something good that we can do.

The Good News to the one who has lost everything is that life does not consist in the things we possess and that every person's life is a plan of God.

The Good News is that we can have abundant lives regardless of the response of other people. As we work with people, we have the grace to love them, even when they may despise us.

Isn't that a beautiful message? We, who have accepted Jesus, are called to share this precious message of salvation with all who will listen.

Holiness

Holiness is a goal that is for everyone, everywhere, to achieve. The writer of the Book of Hebrew tells the importance of holiness, for he says, "Seek to be at peace with all men and to be holy, for without holiness no one will see the Lord" (Hebrews 12:14).

The Old Testament tells us about many people who were used by God to accomplish many wonderful things for His glory. God can use people of all ranks, colors, or of any other classification of mankind, but those who are used of God must be made holy. So, let's pursue this idea of holiness.

From the English dictionary, there are several words that are helpful in understanding this concept. First of all, the word, "*holy*" [ME>OE halig is akin to OE hal, whole], means,

> "...1. **exalted or worthy of complete devotion, as one perfect in goodness and righteousness; 2. divine (as in Ps. 99:9, for the Lord our God is holy); 3. devoted to the deity or the work of the deity (as a temple, or the prophets); 4. having a divine quality....**"

Another word, "*hallow*" [ME halowen>OE halgian>halig, holy], comes from the same word.

Another important word in understanding holiness is the word, "*sanctify*" [ME sanctifien>MF sanctifier>LL sanctificare>Sanctus, sacres], which means,

> "...1. **to set apart to a sacred purpose or to religious use: consecrate; 2. to free from sin: purify; 3. to impart or impute**

sacredness, inviolability, or respect of; 4. to make productive of holiness or piety (as in Deut. 5:12, observe the Sabbath day to sanctify it)...."

A similar word, *"consecrate"* [ME>L consecratus, pp of consecrare>con+sacrare-to consecrate], has the same meaning.

In the Greek, we also have important words to consider. One Greek word, ἅγιος (hagios), means,

"...dedicated, set apart, holy; a. of God, pure, implying distance between the Divine and the profane (John 17:11); b. of things, dedicated to God and His service (Matthew 24:15); c. of persons, dedicated to and thus partaking of the holiness of God (Romans 1:7, Mark 6:20)...."

This word is used 230 times in the New Testament. In the KJV, it is translated, "holy," in reference to the spirit, 89 times; and, it is translated, "saints," in reference to the followers of Jesus, 54 times. For example, in Luke 12:12, we are told that "the *Holy* Spirit will teach you"; in Acts 4:31, the disciples were "filled with the *Holy* Spirit"; in Romans 1:7, the believers are called *"saints"*; in Romans 12:1, we are to present our bodies as a living sacrifice, *"holy* and well-pleasing to God"; in Romans 15:25, Paul was going to Jerusalem to minister to the *"saints"*; and, in Ephesians 1:1, Paul was writing to the *"saints"* in Ephesus.

Another Greek word, ἁγιάζω (hagiazo), is a verb, meaning,

"to sanctify...; a. dedicate, set apart things or persons for God (Matthew 23:17, John 10:36); b. to purify legally or morally (1 Corinthians 6:11, 7:14); c. to cleanse

persons or things ceremonially (Hebrews 9:13, 2 Timothy 2:21); d. to treat as holy, venerate (Matthew 6:9)...."

This word is used 28 times in the New Testament. It is translated as "saints" 25 times, as "hallowed" 2 times, and as "holy" one time. For example, in 1 Corinthians 6:11, Paul reminds the Corinthians that they were in the past living wicked lives, "But you were washed, you were **sanctified**, you were justified in the name of Jesus Christ and by the spirit of our God"; and, in 1 Thessalonians 5:23, Paul says to them, "And may the God of peace himself completely **sanctify** you, and may your spirit, soul, and body be completely kept blameless at the coming of our Lord Jesus Christ."

Concerning holiness, Moses had a life-changing experience with the Eternal one day as he was caring for the sheep of Jethro, his father-in-law. In the midst of his activities as he led the sheep in the desert to Horeb, the mountain of God, the Lord appeared to him in flames of fire within a bush. Moses, seeing that the bush was burning but not being consumed, went closer to examine this strange sight. When he got near the bush, God called Moses by name, saying, "Moses, Moses!" Then, Moses responded by saying, "Here I am" (Exodus 3:1-6).

God had a message for Moses, but first Moses had to realize the holiness of the Eternal, who said, "Do not come any closer. Take off your sandals, for the place where you are standing is holy ground." Then, Moses hid his face, because he was afraid to look at God. Moses was not prepared to serve God until he realized the holiness and magnitude of the Almighty Creator and Sustainer of the universe.

Likewise, we must realize our weakness, because we can do nothing without Him and His grace. But, if we are willing to become His slave, then we can be a blessing to many, and He can even remove mountains that get in the way of our service for Him. It is always an awesome experience to have an encounter with the Almighty. Life is never the same afterwards. God has a job for each of us to do, but we must be holy to qualify for the work of the Lord. For Moses, the job was to lead the Children of Israel out of the land of Egypt.

One of the requirements of holiness is faithful obedience to God. Paul tells us what the works of the flesh are in Galatians 5:19-22, which are "fornication, uncleanness, sensuality, idolatry, abuse of drugs, hostility, strife, jealousy, fits of rage, self-seeking ambition, dissensions, factions, envy, drunkenness, carousing, and the like." The works of the flesh are contrary to the will of God for our lives. To participate in them is to be rebellious against His will and to refuse to receive His holiness for our lives.

Rebellion was the sin that drove Adam and Eve from the Garden of Eden. When they sinned, they were driven from the presence of the God of righteousness. When God created our first ancestors, he gave them everything that they needed to have a good life, but in the garden there was one tree that was forbidden by God for them to eat of its fruit. They chose the desires of the flesh, eating from the forbidden tree, and rebelling against His will. After they sinned against God, guilt dominated their lives. In their unholy relationship to God, they were shamefully embarrassed, and they tried to hide from Him.

Holiness requires us to recognize God's authority. We have the choice to live under the authority of God, which leads to a good, benevolent life of service, or we can live under the authority of Satan, which leads to a bad, dysfunctional life of uselessness. When we follow Jesus, we accept His call for us to take up our cross and commit our lives to serve Him. The Christian life is a life of obedience to Him. That is why Paul referred to himself as "a slave of Jesus." It is good to be a slave of Jesus, because He is the perfect master, and He is always interested in us. His commands are always the best for us, so, it is a privilege to be His slave.

Holiness is also a vital part of spiritual worship. The worship of God is more than a ritual. In Exodus 20:4, we read, "You shall not make for yourself an idol in the form of anything in heaven above or on earth beneath or in the waters below." Jesus told the woman at the well at Sychar in Samaria that "true worshippers will worship the Father in spirit and truth, for such the father seeks to worship him. God is spirit, and those who worship him must worship in spirit and in truth" (John 4:23-24). Then Paul writes to the Romans about the holy sacrifice, saying, "I appeal to you therefore, brothers, by the mercies of God, to present your bodies as a living sacrifice, holy and well-pleasing to God, which is your reasonable service; and do not be conformed to this age, but be transformed by the renewing of the mind, so that you may be able to discern the will of God, which is good, well-pleasing, and perfect " (Romans 12:1-2).

The only way we can worship the true God is in the spirit, because He is spirit. An idol can never be worthy of worship. We must surrender our lives on the altar of service to be capable of worshipping the true and living God. When I have presented my body as a living sacrifice, it becomes a holy sacrifice which is acceptable and is a spiritual service of worship.

When Jesus rode a donkey into the city of Jerusalem on Palm Sunday, the Messianic hopes of the people were then all ablaze with the expectation of immediate realization of the fulfillment of Scripture. However, the Jews were looking for a political leader to sit on a visible throne and to rule the nations by military power. But, Jesus came to reign from an invisible throne through love and compassion, rather than through military strength.

When Jesus arrived at the temple, he was disturbed by what he saw. The temple had been built for spiritual services, but it had been converted into a place of merchandise. The leadership was more interested in making money than for helping those who were seeking the grace of God. After turning over the money-changers' tables and the benches of those selling doves, he said, "It is written, 'My house shall be called the house of prayer,' but you are making it a 'cave of robbers.' " There is no place for robbers in God's place of worship, because God is holy, and those who worship Him must be holy.

Holiness always accompanies genuine prayer. The Psalmist asks the question, "Who may ascend the hill of the Lord? Who may stand in His holy place?" And, the answer is, "He who has clean hands and a pure heart, who does not lift up his soul to an idol or swear by what it false." If our hands are dirty and our hearts are impure, our prayers are in vain (Psalm 24:3-4), but when we cleanse our hands and let Him purify our thoughts, He hears us and answers our prayers.

What do we usually pray for? There are many things that people pray for, such as a job with more pay, better health, a life of happiness, deliverance from an addiction, forgiveness of sin, welfare of a friend, peace for our nation and the world. Do we pray to convince God to change His plans for us and our friends? These prayers are common and natural.

Might it not be a more spiritual plan to pray to find out about what His plans are for us and for our friends? When we find out what His plans are, we might then start asking Him to change us. So, when I pray, I should be more concerned about me changing my thoughts and actions and less about me changing His thoughts and actions. If I know where He is going, I can amend my ways and follow Him. If my hands are dirty, I need to clean them; and, if my heart is impure, it needs to be purified. I can clean my hands by changing my lifestyle; and, I can surrender myself to the Lord, and he will cleanse my heart. If I have the sins of hostility and ill will toward others, I can forgive them, and God will forgive me of my sins against Him. Our main prayer must be, "Lord, forgive me of my sins!" Then, we can pray, "Here I am, send me!" Then, He will have a job for me to do. Prayer and holiness work together.

Another characteristic of holiness is joyful service. The Greek words for joy and grace come from the same Greek word. You cannot have the one without the other. When people come to the Lord for salvation, they are flooded with the joy that comes with it. The experience of Zacchaeus well illustrates this point. Jesus encountered this man one day as he went through Jericho. Zacchaeus was a rich man who was chief of the tax collectors. He was small in height, so he ran and climbed up into a fig-mulberry tree so he could see Jesus as he passed by. Jesus, seeing him, approached the tree where he was, and, looking up, He said, "Zacchaeus, come down quickly, for I must go to your house today." In response, Zacchaeus came down quickly and received him joyfully. Jesus said, "Today salvation has come to this house" (Luke 19:1-10).

Paul was a Pharisee and a persecutor of the church, and with vengeance, he tried to destroy it. When he was commissioned to go to Damascus to persecute the church there, he had an experience with the Lord Jesus Christ that changed his life. On that day, he surrendered his life to the Lord. The Lord took his cold, murderous heart and changed it into a benevolent, compassionate heart.

Paul lost his power and status among the Pharisees, but he received more than he lost. He wrote to the Philippians (3:7-9) and said,

> *"(7) But those things that were gain for me I have counted them as a loss for the sake of Christ. (8) Yes, I also count all things a loss in view of the surpassing knowledge of Christ Jesus my Lord, on account of whom I have suffered loss of all things; and I consider them to be refuse in order that I may gain Christ (9) and to be found in him, not having my righteousness of the law, but through faith in Christ, the righteousness of God based on faith...."*

To be holy means that we have surrendered our lives to God and that we are now His servants. We have been separated from the works of the flesh, so we can enjoy the fruit of the Spirit. Now we have a new nature, because the old has passed away.

In Romans 12:1-2, it is written,

> *"(1)...to present your bodies as a living sacrifice, holy and well-pleasing to God, which is your reasonable service; (2) and do not be conformed to this age, but be transformed by the renewing of the mind, so that you may be able to discern the will*

of God, which is good, well-pleasing, and
perfect."

So, it is not possible to worship God if there is no holiness.

After we have been purified, we are prepared for a joyous life of service. He gives us the ministry of reconciliation. Our sins have been blotted out, so we do not live in sin and disgrace anymore. We have become children of the King and heirs to His Kingdom, and we have the message of salvation to share with the world.

Jesus Loves the Lost
(Luke 15:1-32)

In the 14th chapter of Luke Jesus tells us about the cost of discipleship, teaching us that if we cannot say farewell to all our possessions, we cannot be his disciple. He was demanding a complete surrender (Luke 14:33).

We are informed about the ones following Jesus: tax collectors, sinners, Pharisees, and scribes. Some were following for good reasons, but others were harsh fault finders. Let us examine those who were following Jesus.

The Greek word for tax collector is τελώνης, which means revenue officer or toll collector. In the NT they were unpopular Jewish subordinates who hired out to foreign officials holding tax collecting contracts.

The word for sinner in Greek is ἀμαρτωλός, meaning sinful, guilty, shown to be wrong, one who lives in opposition to the divine will.

The Greek word for Pharisee is φαρισαῖος, one who is set apart, separatist, a member or follower of the sect of the Pharisees, an organized society of Jews who claimed authority in interpreting the Scriptures and setting rules for the observance of the law in daily life.

The word for Scribe is Greek is γραμματεύς, one skilled in Jewish law and theology, expert, scholar, a town official secretary, town clerk.

Jesus was popular among the tax collectors and the sinners, but the Pharisees and the teachers of the law were critical of Jesus. They thought that it was disgusting for Jesus to eat with sinners—and he even welcomed them to be his friends! The critics thought this association with sinners lowered the standard of God's people and made the one who "stooped so low" to be unholy and a bad example for others to emulate. The Pharisees and lawyers were only interested in working with the "good" people. Jesus came to minister to everyone—especially the lost!

In our text, the 15th chapter of Luke, the major concern is about our responsibility to rescue the sinners from their lost condition. So, Jesus told them about lost things. All the tax collectors and sinners were eager to hear Jesus teach, but the Pharisees and Scribes were finding fault with Jesus. They were greatly murmuring against Jesus. There are two Greek words used for murmuring: διαγογγύζω, as in expressing dissatisfaction, to complain, grumble (aloud), mutter; and, γογγύζω, as in expressing dissatisfaction, to grumble, murmur, as expressing skepticism about someone, to mutter, complain secretly, speak in a low voice, whisper. In Luke 15:2, they were no longer whispering about it, but now they are boldly condemning Jesus for welcoming the tax collectors and eating with them. This word is used in only one other place. It was when Jesus accepted the invitation to eat with Zacchaeus (Luke 19:1-9).

In telling about lost things in the first part of chapter 15, Luke records the parable of the lost sheep. The Greek word for parable is παραβολή, meaning the placing of one thing by the side of another, a comparing, a short relation under which something else is figured, or in which that which is fictitious is employed to represent people rather than about sheep or other things, that which is real. It is an earthly story with a heavenly message. In the story of the lost sheep, one sheep in a flock of a hundred went away, perhaps by careless wandering, and it was rescued by the good shepherd. This is a story about a shepherd who searched until he found it, but the message was about the lost who repented and was saved. Luke summed it up in verse 7: "I tell you, there will likewise be more joy in heaven over one repentant sinner than over ninety-nine righteous people who have no need of repentance."

Next in Luke 15, Jesus tells us about a woman who had ten silver coins. She loses one, and she lights a lamp and sweeps the house and seeks carefully until she finds the lost coin. After she finds it, she calls together her friends and neighbors and says, "Rejoice with me, because I found my silver coin that was lost." Jesus then says, "Likewise, I tell you, there is joy before the angels of God over one repentant sinner." In this parable we see that the lost coin is the story but the real message is about the lost sinner being found.

Then, in Luke 15:11, the story of the Prodigal Son begins. The younger of two brothers wanted to leave home. Perhaps he thought that the restrictions were too binding. His desire was to get away from home with the rules and regulations of the "old-fashioned" ideas of his father. His interest turned toward finding himself and showing the world how important he really was. He wanted to get very far away from home with all its restrictions, which involved such things as honest work and moral living.

The younger brother asked his father for his share in his inheritance, early. He wanted it "now," so the father divided the estate for him. In a few days, he left to go into a faraway country. His pockets were full, and his arrogance was evident. The geographical distance from the father was not as important as the emotion distance. He had cut the string that attached him to his father's house; indeed, he had been liberated. Now he could choose his own companions and his own lifestyle.

In that faraway country, the younger son lived recklessly, and he scattered his money living prodigally. The

Greek word for prodigally is ἀσότος (asotos). It comes
from the word, σώζω (sozo), which means to save. The α
before the word means that it is a privation, giving it the
negative meaning of the word. It is an adverb that means
"one who cannot be saved." He was a spendthrift, an
abandoned man, a prodigal. The English word, prodigal,
comes from a Latin word meaning, "exceedingly or
recklessly wasteful."

It was not long before the younger brother had
squandered all his wealth. He was then in desperate need of
money and faraway from home. In the parable, the father is
God, and the prodigal is the lost sinner. When the sinner
goes faraway from God, he becomes desperate, without
hope in this world or the next. In his riotous living, he had
exhausted his body, debased his mind, destroyed his wealth,
and damned his soul. In his desperation, he sought to find
someone who would help him.

The Prodigal was joined to a citizen of that faraway
country. Actually, the Greek word was κολλάο (kollao),
which means "glued to the man." The verb is a passive
voice, which means that he was "glued together or cleaved
to that citizen." The man gave him the job of feeding swine,
which was the most degrading occupation known to the
Jews. He was living with the pigs. The hogs were eating the
κερατίων (keration), which were the pods of the carob tree,
whose sweet tasting pods were shaped like little horns. He
wanted to eat the food of the pigs, but no one gave him
anything.

The Prodigal finally came to himself. He had left
home with a pompous step of an exaggerated show of his
self-importance; but, now his money was gone and his fair-
weather friends had left him. His stomach was empty, and
he had no way to satisfy his gnawing hunger. So, there

among the swine, with a bruised self-image, a disappointed heart, and a hungry stomach, he found himself. God has a way of getting our attention. Oftentimes, we do not hear His voice when everything seems to be going our way. So he takes away the flashy atmosphere and the boisterous noises, and with dead silence, He communicates with us.

There in the atmosphere of the grunting swine that were wallowing in the mud, he began to realize that there might be a better lifestyle than this. He remembered that his father had many hired servants and that they had an abundance of bread; but he, on the other hand, had no bread, and he was starving to death. With a repentant heart, he arose to go back to the Father's house. In his restless toil, he prepared a speech to make when he met his Father: "Father, I have sinned against heaven and before you. I am no longer worthy to be called your son. Make me as one of your hired servants." So, he began to travel on the long road back home.

When the Prodigal came in sight of the Father's house, the Father saw him. This was the time the Father had been waiting for. He was moved with compassion. The Greek word is ἐσπλαγχίσθη (esplagchnisthe). This is a beautiful word. It is from the word, σπλάγχνον (spagchnon), which means "the viscera or chief intestines." It is used 12 times, and it is always translated in English as "compassion." It is the combination of the Latin, "con" (with) and "passion" (intensive passion). It is the "gut feeling," and it is an emotion that calls for action. Without it nothing great will happen.

When the father reached the son, it was a wonderful sight to behold. The Father embraced him and kissed him. The word used is καταφιλέω (kataphileo). The word, φιλέω (phileo), means "to love." When the prefix, κατά (kata), is added to the word, it means "to kiss fervently or affectionately," and when it is in the imperfect tense, it means "repeatedly." So, while the Prodigal was still far away, his father saw him and was moved with compassion. Running to him, he fell upon his neck and fervently and repeatedly kissed him.

The Prodigal began his speech of repentance and submission, but the father was not interested in hearing it, because he was ready to celebrate. He said to his slaves, "Quickly! Bring out the best robe and put it around him, and put a signet ring on his hand and sandals on his feet. Bring and kill the fatted calf" (Luke 15:22-23). It was such a momentous event that it was appropriate for the celebration party to begin immediately.

It was not just a robe that the father called for, but it was the best robe that was put around the son who had come home. The signet ring meant that he was his father's assistant. It was like giving the family checkbook to him, because the ring gave him authority to make purchases. He put sandals on his feet, which was a sign for the slaves to accept him as master. Then he told them to bring that young fat calf to be slaughtered for the feast. It was not just any calf. It was the one that had been grain fed. The father had been preparing for the expected homecoming of the prodigal, and now it had happened. The father said, "For this my son was dead and now he is alive again, he was lost and he has been found" (Luke 15:24). The slaughter of the fatted calf was the height of hospitality.

Then, the party began. Actually, the word was εὐφαίνομαι (euphainomai), meaning "to make glad, celebrate, be jubilant." The return of the Prodigal was a very appropriate time to celebrate by "merrymaking."

Upon returning from the field and approaching the house, the elder brother heard music, συμφωνίας (sumphonias), and dances, χορὸν (choron). The word for music means "sounding together," hence, as a concert of instruments. It is the combination of the word, φωνή (phone), meaning "the production of a sound," and the prefix, συμ (sum), which together means "to sound with or together."

This use of the word, χορός, is the only place it is used in the New Testament. It is in the plural form, so it means "dances."

The father's celebration of the Prodigal's return home must have been a very joyous occasion. The harmony of the music caught the ear of the elder brother. So, he called one of the lads to inquire what was happening. The lad said, "Your brother has come, and your father killed the fatted calf because he is back and in good health" (Luke 15:27).

This made the elder brother very angry, and he refused to come in. The father came out to plead with him, but he responded by saying, "Lo, these many years I have served you and I have never disobeyed your orders, and you have never given me a goat to celebrate with my friends. But when this son of yours, who has squandered your property living with prostitutes, comes home, you killed for him the fatted calf!" (Luke 15:29-30).

The father replied, "Son, you are always with me, and everything I have is yours. But we had to celebrate and rejoice because this brother of yours was dead, but now he lives. He was lost but he was found" (Luke 15:31-32). The father said, "this brother of yours," but the son said, "this son of yours." The father tried to show the elder brother that the Prodigal was his brother, but the elder brother would not acknowledge that the Prodigal was his brother.

The parable was told to the Pharisees, teachers of the law, tax collectors, and sinners. The Pharisees and lawyers thought they were too holy to eat with tax collectors and sinners. They did not want to be contaminated by touching those who were the "dregs of society"!

The parable of the Prodigal Son has a message for this modern day as well as for that day. We still have people who take the attitude of the elder brother. What do we celebrate about? Are we more excited about our promotions than seeing the prodigal come home? Are we more thrilled about our favorite team winning the game than seeing the lost restored? Are we more interested in associating with our own social equal than getting dirty by touching the prodigal? Are we more interested in going to the banquets of the rich and famous than in making merry with the poor sinner who comes home?

Jesus came to seek and to save the lost. He was criticized for eating with the social outcast. There are two kinds of sinners: those who have been saved by grace and those who are still alienated from God. Are we identified with the elder brother or are we identified with the younger brother? Where do you stand? Do we have the warm compassion of the Father when the sinner comes home? The mature Christian always rejoices when the lost is found. It is a thrill that exceeds the pay raise, the promotion, winning the game, or any other thing that this world offers. It is beholding the coming in of the Kingdom of God. When the father invites you to come in to the celebration, accept his invitation, which goes beyond all expectations. You will always be glad you made that eternal decision. Blessings on you!

Jesus, The Messiah

Christmas, the season of all seasons, is about here again. Some are actually trying to change the name of the season, using terms such as "Season's Holiday," or some other non-descriptive expression to divert from the real meaning of the season. But, to me, and I assume to you, it will always be Christmas, which commemorates the birth of our Savior.

Luke and Matthew are the only Gospel writers who tell us about the birth of Jesus. Luke tells us about Jesus being born in Bethlehem, with the message coming to the shepherds; Matthew tells us about the wise men from the East coming to worship the newborn king. In Luke's account, Jesus is a baby; in Matthew's account, Jesus is a little boy about two years old. In Luke, we see Jesus in a manger; in Matthew, we see Jesus in the house with his mother.

It was the angel who named Jesus. The angel appeared to Joseph in a dream and said, "Joseph, son of David, do not fear to take Mary as your wife. It is by the Holy Spirit that she has conceived this child. She will bear a son, and you shall call his name Jesus, for he will save his people from their sins!" (Matthew 1:20-21). So, the name of Jesus is the name that is above all names. Paul writes to the Philippians that "...God highly exalted him and gave him the name that is above every name. So that at the name of Jesus every knee should bow, in heaven and on the earth and under the earth, and every tongue shall acknowledge that Jesus Christ is Lord, to the glory of God the Father" (Philippians 2:9-11).

The names, Jesus and Joshua, come from the same Hebrew word: יְשׁוּעַ הַמָּשִׁיחַ, which means, "Jesus the Messiah." The Greek word is Ἰησοῦν (Iesun). And, in English, it is Jesus, the Christ, which means "The Anointed." Kings and priests were anointed when they took their place of authority. So, there were many who were anointed. For hundreds of years, the prophets prophesied that The Anointed was coming. The Jews were looking for an anointed one who would be a warrior and who would lead the people of Israel to a military victory that would give them liberty and supremacy. The Anointed One did come, but He was not interested in wielding the sword for military victory. He was far greater than they expected. Jesus was the one that came from God. He had the power to forgive sins, and he was for all the nations, not just for the Jews.

Yes, Jesus is the name above all other names. It means "salvation," and it is used 917 times in the New Testament. The name of Jesus was so powerful that the high priest and the council commanded the apostles saying, "We strictly charged you not to teach in this name, and behold you have filled Jerusalem with your teaching, and you intend to make us guilty of this man's blood" (Acts 5:28). As their spokesman, Peter answered, "We must obey God rather than men."

The apostles were released, but they continued to preach in the name of Jesus, and they were brought before the council again. After beating them, the council charged them not to speak in the name of Jesus. The apostles left the council rejoicing, because they were deemed worthy to suffer shame for the name. Everyday in the temple and from house to house, they did not cease teaching and preaching that Jesus is the Christ.

When Jesus was born in Bethlehem of Judea in the days of Herod the king, wise men came from the East to Jerusalem, saying, "Where is the newborn king of the Jews. For we saw his star in the East, and have come to worship him." They were searching to find Jesus. Their search was mysterious and enthusiastic. They thought that Jerusalem was the Holy City and the place for the newborn king. They came a long way, and their search only veered off the target to the North by a few miles.

The wise men did not know that talking about a new king was dangerous talk in the hearing of Herod the king. When Herod heard about the birth of a new king, he was troubled, and the whole city of Jerusalem with him. Herod was troubled to hear about anyone who would take his place as king. The people were troubled, because they knew about the atrocious nature of Herod. He had killed many who were in line to be king. He even killed those of his own household. The city trembled, because they feared that Herod would do bad things in Jerusalem.

So, Herod called together all the chief priests and scribes of the people, and he inquired from them where the Christ was to be born. They knew the Scriptures, so they told him that he was to be born in Bethlehem of Judah.

Herod called the wise men and accurately ascertained the exact time of the appearing of the star. Herod was a deceitful liar when he said, "As you go, search diligently for the child. When you have found him report to me so I can go and worship him." We know that Herod was not interested in worshiping the new king; he was only interested in killing him.

After the audience with Herod, the star they had seen in the East went before them until it stood over the place where the child was. They were filled with emotions; they rejoiced with exceeding great joy. When they came to the house, they saw the child with his mother, and they fell down and worshipped him. Jesus was no longer a baby; he as a little boy, one or two years old. They opened their treasures and presented him gifts of gold, frankincense, and myrrh.

It was revealed to them that Herod was a fake. So, they did not return to Herod, but they went to their own country another way.

When Herod saw that he was outwitted by the wise men, he was in a furious rage. He would seek to find the child Jesus and kill him. God is never outwitted. He revealed to Joseph what was about to happen. He was told in a dream, "Get up and take the child and his mother and go to Egypt, and stay there until I tell you, for Herod is going to search for the child to destroy him." The Holy Family was in Egypt until Herod died.

Herod did try to find Jesus, but to no avail. He had much power, and he had murdered many people to stay in power, but now he was dealing with the Almighty. In his frustration, he killed all the male children in Bethlehem and its vicinity who were two years old and under, according to the time which he had learned from the wise men.

Life is still the same. Those who seek the Lord with all their hearts will find Him, and when they do, they will find exceeding great joy in Him. It is God's grace that blesses us. Those who trust Him are protected from all anxieties and worries. On the other hand, the wicked are like the restless sea that never finds peace and rest. Those who fight against God are always losers; those who serve the Master are the blessed. You make the choice. I pray that you make the choice to go with Jesus. Then, your life will be

secure and meaningful here and prepared for eternity.
Blessings on you!

יֵשׁוּעַ הַמְשִׁיחַ

Joy

Joy is a beautiful word, and it is a most precious gift to those who have it. It is greater than happiness, because joy is a present reality; happiness is determined by circumstances. If we go to the doctor and he tells us that all the parts of the physical body are working as they should, that is news that gives us feelings of happiness.

If we should, all of a sudden, be given a million dollars, regardless if it should come from an inheritance, or the lottery, or any other way, we would be happy and probably be jumping around in glee and happiness.

Happiness is a wonderful feeling that we can have, but it is still determined by circumstances. Joy, on the other hand, is of a different caliber. It is associated with a divine relationship with the eternal. The Greek word for *joy* is χαρά (chara). Both χαρά and its related word, χαρίς (charis), meaning "*grace*," are from the same root, χάρ (char). Joy is related to grace about like grace is related to gracious, or joy is to joyous. You cannot have the one without having the other.

Joy is one of the attributes of the Fruit of the Spirit, the first three of which are Love, Joy, and Peace (Galatians 5:23). They come together in a cluster. We receive them by *grace*, through *faith*. So, grace is the source of salvation; *joy* is the abiding presence.

Since happiness is contingent on circumstances, it is temporal, enduring for only a time. "Happiness" comes from the word, "hap," implying by luck or chance, and its derivation is: {from ME hap, earlier happe, from the Old Norse happ, good luck}.

Joy, on the other hand, is eternal and does not depend on circumstance. Joy has the meaning of great pleasure or delight, and its derivation is: {from ME joi<Ofr. > Lat.gaudia<gaudere, to rejoice}.

So, if the one who has this joy, which is an attribute of the Fruit of the Spirit, goes to the doctor and is told that his/her bodily symptoms are due to organs that have quit functioning and that the future is dim, even so, the joy of salvation is still evident.

If our bank account is overdrawn, and there is no way to replenish it, and the bills are overdue, yet, joy is still with us, because "We know that all things work together for good to those loving God, who are called according to his purpose" (Romans 8:28).

Even in the time of disaster, the first 3 attributes of the Fruit of the Spirit, Love, Joy, and Peace, are evident. Happiness may be gone, but joy and grace are still our companions.

Even though Salvation is a permanent relationship to God, it can be dulled by the works of the flesh.   Even though the disciple of Jesus has been "saved by grace through faith," he/she still lives in a body of flesh, and the flesh calls out for satisfaction.

The Fruit of the Spirit and the works of the flesh are opposite to one another. They are like light vs. darkness; truth vs. falsehood; cold vs. hot; good vs. bad; love vs. hate; joy vs. sorrow; peace vs. war. To have the one precludes the possibility of having the other.

By contrast to the Fruit of the Spirit, the first 3 attributes in the list of the works of the flesh are fornication, uncleanness, and sensuality. Fornication, along with the other two attributes, is physical license without responsibility. In God's plan, sex is pure and holy, and in his purpose after he created Adam and Eve, they became one— the consummation of physical union.   In marriage, the intimate relationship is a beautiful expression of unity, but perverted sex is unholy and destroys a compatible relationship between two people, whether hetero- or homosexual. Marriage can become a curse rather than a blessing. Just two people having a relationship with one another can never bring joy and peace, because it is a pseudo-love, a relationship that has never been blessed by the Almighty.

The Greek words, ἔρος (eros), and ἀγάπη (agape), are both translated into English as "love." One is a physical attraction, and the other is an esteem for another. Ἔρος is a pseudo-love; ἀγάπη is a genuine love. The first is as different from the second as fleshly pleasure is to committed responsibility and as the works of the flesh are to the Fruit of the Spirit.

Worry, even though it is not listed in Paul's catalogue of "the works of the flesh," is included in the phrase, "and the like," as also mentioned in Galatians 5:21. When Paul had finished his list, he realized that the list was too great to include everything; so, he wrote that there are others like those specifically mentioned. I consider that worry is one of them.

We receive **grace** and **joy** through **faith**, and faith is not only the initial way of receiving grace, but it becomes a way of life for us. Therefore, it is very important that we live by faith daily. Faith is the means of salvation, and it is also the means of **sanctification**. To grow in grace, we must live by faith.

Someone may say, "You do not understand my problems. Worry is the way I handle my anxieties in depressive circumstances." My answer is, "Worry is contrary to faith, and when we live by worry, we are not living by grace. Even though we may be living under heavy burdens, worry is not the answer. It may be financial burdens, social failures, or health problems, but it is no time to exchange faith for worry."

Whatever our problems, grace finds a way out; worry compounds them. If we have no money, we can still store up treasures in heaven. If our health is gone and we are told by the doctor that the end is near, worry will compound the problem, but grace finds a way out. We are all facing the last day. Time is precious if we only know how to use it— whether short or long. Again, worry compounds the problem, but grace and faith give us a more mature way of looking at time and eternity. The works of the flesh bring worry, but the Fruit of the Spirit produces joy.

The third attribute of the Fruit of the Spirit is **peace**, which is intimately associated with both love and joy. Paul, in the fifth chapter of Romans sums up what he has said in the four previous chapters concerning faith. He says, "Now that we have been justified by faith, we have peace with God through our Lord Jesus Christ" (Romans 5:1).

Much has been said about peace, but we still have bloody wars. The fourth chapter of the Book of James asks the question of the source of fights and quarrels. James answers his question by saying that it is because of the evil desires of our hearts. The battle rages in our hearts, because we want more, which leads to covetousness and murder.

The way to peace is through the provisions of God. James says, "Submit yourselves therefore to God. Resist the devil, and he will flee from you. Draw near to God, and he will draw near to you. Cleanse your hands, you sinners, and purify your hearts, you double-minded" (James 4:7-8).

The works of the flesh are diametrically opposed to peace. Selfish ambition, hostility, jealousy, covetousness, grudges, and hatreds never lead to peace. We see it exemplified in the family when there is sibling against sibling, and children against parents. It is only through God's grace that peace comes to the family. Without God's gift of grace and compassion, members of the same family sometimes become bitter and hostile toward one another and harbor grudges for a lifetime. What a tragedy!

Where are you today? Do you have the *joy* that goes beyond all human understanding? It should be ours, and if we do not have it, we can be assured that it is available for us now, today.

We cannot have joy if we harbor hostility and ill will. We must live in the habit of forgiveness. We need to be forgiven, and we cannot be forgiven unless we forgive others. So, the cost for forgiveness of our sins is to live with compassion and forgiveness of others. To live with joy and grace is to live with compassion and forgiveness. It is like the difference between light and darkness, truth and falsehood. Holding to one excludes the other. So, what shall it be?

I vote for joy and grace.

Love

Love is an Old English word used with a variety of meanings. We use it to express many of our emotions, for example, in such expressions as, "I love my house; I love my spouse; I love my coffee; I love my neighbor; I love my dog!" We also use many more phrases to express our feelings, but how would we define Love? We would perhaps use such synonyms as "affection, fondness, adoration, friendliness, appreciation, admiration, or esteem."

The Hebrew people also had words that were used in a variety of ways. The Hebrew word, אהב (ahab), means "to have affections for (sexually, or otherwise), to love, to like, or friend." They had another word, רחם (raw-kham), which means "to fondle, to love, have compassion, show mercy, and have pity." Yet another very important word in the Hebrew language, חסד (gheh-sed), is translated in the KJV Bible as "mercy, kindness, goodness, favor, and loving-kindness." The word is used 218 times, and it is usually translated as "mercy"; however, it is translated as "loving-kindness" 31 times.

The Greek language has four words that express different aspect of the emotion that we call "love" in English. The Greek words are ἔρος (eros), στοργός (storgos), φίλος (philos), and ἀγάπη (agape). The word ἔρος is not used in the New Testament, but it is used several times in the Greek translation of the Old Testament.

The word ἔρος was used in Greek mythology for the god of love, son of Aphrodite; it was also identified by the Romans as Cupid. In the Greek language, this type of "love" seeks others for the fulfillment of his/her own sexual desires. The English word "erotic" is from this word. Although this emotion exhibits a very powerful urge for a person to satisfy his/her sexual desire, it is not enough to make a lasting commitment in marriage. It is like a person who has a gnawing desire to satisfy the desires of the flesh, for example, the habit of smoking cigarettes. When the person has sucked up the smoke of the 20 cigarettes, he/she throws the package away. That is what happens in a promiscuous relationship. Boy and girl "fall in love," but if ἔρος is all they have, it will not be very long until they "fall out of love." They love one another so long as they meet one another's psychological needs, but when they cease to do that, the "love" fades and falls away. The only interest with ἔρος is in fulfilling one's own fleshly desires. That is no basis for a permanent relationship. It is enough to bring the new creation of a child into the world; but, it is not enough to give that new creation a mature family life where a stable and blessed environment is provided to grow up in.

In the book of Hosea, we learn about the prophet Hosea and his love affair with Gomer. They were married and had three children. Then, Gomer left Hosea, and she went after lovers of the flesh (Hosea 2:13; 3:1). Hosea had a deeper love than ἔρος. He loved her after she had lost her virtue. Gomer lost her self-respect, and her beauty faded. She actually had become a slave. When she was auctioned off to the highest bidder, Hosea bought her back for fifteen shekels of silver and one and a half homer of barley, which was the price of a slave. Ἔρος is the beautiful gift of the marriage bed, but God will judge the fornicator.

Another Greek word for love is στοργός (storgos). It is the love of family, so it is usually translated as "natural affection." The negative, or opposite, of the word is ἀστόργους, and it is used 2 times in the New Testament (Romans 1:31 & 2 Timothy 3:3), with both times being translated as "without natural affection." It describes the awful condition of the Romans in the day of Jesus.

Not only is στοργός an instinct given to humans, but the animals of the jungle are endowed with this power of family love. The wild animals, as well as the tame animals, have it as a part of their natural being. Without it, we could not survive as humans; neither could animals survive without it. By this kind of love, the birds of the air protect their young with diligence, and the mother chicken hen embraces her little ones by putting them under her wings. By my own experience of growing up on a farm, I have observed how this kind of love is seen in the behavior of the farm animals. I remember how it was especially dangerous to be around a sow hog when she had piglets with her in her pen. She was eager to protect her little ones, and if anyone was reckless enough to get too close to the sow's piglets, he/she might be in danger of losing an arm or a leg.

In his letter to the Romans, Paul described the condition of the Romans. He emphasized the depravity of the Romans by saying that they were without a natural affection for the young (ἀστόργους). We, as a nation, have also fallen to that low moral caliber. We read about the Egyptians who killed the male babes of the Hebrew children, and we say that was terrible, and it was! But, we have become more depraved than they were, because we kill our own babies and then go on our own way, refusing to accept the guilt and shame that goes with it.

Φίλος (philos) is another important word for love. It is defined as "a friend, or having tender affection, or being intimate." The word is used 29 times in the New Testament, and it is translated as "friend" in every reference in the KJV. Jesus is called the *friend* of publicans and sinners. In the parable of the lost sheep, when the shepherd had found the lost sheep, he called in his *friends* to tell them of the good news about finding the lost sheep. We share our lives with our friends. James tells us (James 4:4) that if we are a *friend* of the world, we are an enemy of God. Jesus told his disciples, "I have called you *friends*; for all that I have heard from by Father, I have made known to you" (John 15:15).

Some other Greek words use this word, φίλος, to make other words. Some examples are, φιλόστοργος (philostorgos), meaning "kindley affectioned"; φιλοσοφία (philosophia), meaning "love of wisdom"; φιλόθεος, (philotheos), meaning "love of God"; φιλόξενος (philoxenos), meaning "love of the stranger"; φιλάδελφος (philadelphos), meaning "love of brother." The verb form of the word, φιλέω (phileoo), is normally translated "to love." However, in Matthew 26:48, Mark 14:44, and Luke 22:47, it is translated "to kiss." The word is used 25 times in the New Testament, and it is filled with emotional content.

The last Greek word for love, in the verb form, is ἀγαπάω (agapaoo), meaning "I love." It is the kind of love that has "esteem" for another. It is used 143 times in the New Testament. The noun form of the word, ἀγάπη (agape), is used 116 times; the adjective form, ἀγαπητός (agapetos), meaning "beloved" or "dear," is used 61 times. When we include all three forms of the word, it is used a total of 320 times in the New Testament.

The noun, ἀγάπη, is usually translated "love" in the KJV; however, it is translated "charity" 28 times. Ten of those occurrences are found in 1 Corinthians 13:1-13. Paul tells us that if we do not have "charity," we become harsh and sound like clanging brass; if we do not have "charity," but have enough faith to remove mountains, we are nothing; and, if we do not have "charity," but if we deliver our bodies that we may boast, we are profited nothing.

᾿Aγάπη is also the first attribute of the fruit of the Spirit (Galatians 5:23), and we are instructed to be rooted and grounded in this kind of love. To know the ἀγάπη of Christ goes beyond all human understanding. It is the basis of the Gospel of Jesus. Without it we have no message; without it we have no salvation; without it we have no future! When we surrender our lives to the Lord Jesus Christ, we receive the gift of love that is more precious than silver or gold. It supersedes the material world as much as the light supersedes darkness, or as wisdom supersedes folly.

᾿Aγαπάω, the verb, meaning "I love," is the companion word with the noun, ἀγάπη. We are to ἀγαπάω our neighbor as ourselves, and we are to love even our enemies. The verb form is always translated as "love" in the KJV.

Some have said that ἀγαπάω is the "God kind" of love. It is usually used in a good sense, but that is not always the case. In John 3:16, we read, "For God so **loved** the world that he gave his only begotten Son that everyone believing in him may not perish but have eternal life." Then, skipping down to verse 19, we read, "This is the condemnation, for the light has come into the world and men **loved** darkness rather than the light, for their deeds were evil." We also read in the first epistle of John in chapter 2 and verse 15, "Do not **love** the world or the things in the world. If anyone **loves** the world, the **love** of the father is not in him." God loved the world, so he sent his son; the evil men loved darkness, because their deeds were evil. If we love the world, the love of the father is not in us. In 1 John 2:15, the words for "love" are the same; also, the words translated "love" in John 3:16 and John 3:19 are the same. So, sometimes the word is used in a good way, and other times it is used in a bad way. I think that the English word, "esteem," is the best word that translates the meaning of ἀγαπάω.

In John 21:15-17, we clearly see how ἀγάπη is used with the double meaning of the word. When Jesus met with his disciples on the Sea of Galilee after the resurrection, he asked Peter where his loyalty was. In verse 15, Jesus used ἀγάπας (agapas) when he asked him that penetrating question. Then, when he asked him the third time, Jesus used the other word for love, φιλεῖς. That is why Peter was grieved. He was not grieved because Jesus asked him three times, but he was grieved because he used the friendship word for love the third time. We may have hundreds of people that we esteem; but, we only have a few people that are our friends. So, when Jesus put the question on an intimate personal level, Peter was grieved.

In 1 Corinthians 13, the "love chapter," we further see the importance of the 'αγάπη "love or esteem." In 1 Corinthians 13:1, it teaches that if one should speak in tongues, whether it is with ecstatic speech or the eloquence of oratory, it is no good if it is not accompanied with esteem. If the speaker does not have ἀγάπη (esteem) for the recipients of his message, he will be like a sounding gong or a tinkling cymbal.

The Greek word for sound, ἠχών (echon), is our word "echo." In Luke 21:25, it is translated, "the roaring of the sea and the waves." The Greek word for "tinkling" is ἀλαλάζον (alalazon), which means to raise the war cry, "alala," hence to utter loud sounds or to wail (Mark 5:38). So, if we do not have ἀγάπη, the sound of our tongues rattles like a big "gong."

The chapter goes on to say that if I have the gift of prophecy and know all things belonging to the work of salvation, and if I have all knowledge and the gift of teaching, but if I do not have ἀγάπη, I am nothing. Also, if I give all my possessions away, and even deliver my body for martyrdom, but do not have esteem for others, I have no profit.

Then, in 1 Corinthians 13:4-13, ἀγάπη is first characterized in a negative sense. It is not jealous or boastful; it is not arrogant or rude; it does not insist on its own way; it is not irritable or resentful; and, it does not rejoice at wrong.

Then, it is characterized in a positive way. It is patient and kind; it rejoices in the right; it rejoices with the truth; it roofs over all things; it has faith for all things; it hopes in all things; and it endures all things.

Love never falls in ruins; it has a maturity that is adequate for all the trials of life, and it prepares us for death. The chapter closes by saying that πίστις (faith), ἐλπίς (hope), and ἀγάπη remain, but ἀγάπη is the greatest.

Redeeming The Time

A very important message of the scriptures is that as spokesmen for the Gospel, we should be addressing efforts toward "Redeeming the time." By this is meant that we as servants of the Lord must do everything within our power to use what time we have been given to be effective ambassadors of the message of the Gospel to the world.

In the Greek, the word that describes this idea is ἐξαγοράζω (exagorazo), which means, "to buy back, buy up, deliver, make the best use of, or take advantage of." This word is used 4 times in the New Testament, found in Galatians 3:13, Galatians 4:5, Ephesians 5:16, and Colossians 4:5. The word was used in a cultural setting of 2 thousand years ago, but it still has an Eternal message for us in the present day. It is instructive to take a closer look at each of these passages.

In the first of these passages, Galatians 3:13, we are told that "Christ redeemed us from the law by becoming a curse for us." No one can perfectly keep the law, so that means that we are all under the curse of the law. However, Jesus came to deliver us from that curse and to make us free to have victory in righteousness.

In Galatians 4:4-5, we are told that "God sent forth his son, born of a woman, under the law, in order the He might redeem those under the law so that we might receive adoption under the law." So, we are adopted as sons of God, and we receive the Holy Spirit in our hearts and are no longer slaves, but sons and heirs of His glory.

Ephesians 5:15-16 admonishes us, "…be careful how you walk, not as unwise but as wise, redeeming the time, because the days are evil." Even though the days are filled with evil, we can redeem them, buying them back to be used for good things. Thus, we are not to be led astray by the foolishness of evil, but we are to understand what the will of God is for our lives. We are not to be drunk with wine, but we are to be filled with the Holy Spirit. We are never to be influenced by liquor, but to always be influenced by the Spirit of God. Then, we can encourage one another and give thanks to the Lord, always.

In Colossians 4:5, we are reminded that we are to "Walk in wisdom before the outsiders, redeeming the time." We are redeeming the time when we are giving our testimony of walking in righteousness before the world.

What is our concept of "time"? What does it mean to us? First of all, it is the system of sequential events that, in relation to one another, have a past, a present, or a future. In our experience, time has a finite duration, as contrasted with eternity. It has a particular or definite point associated with it, as when indicated by a clock. I'm sure that you would agree that we are all involved with time.

We also use time to measure most everything that we do. For example, we are told that light travels at the speed of 186,282 miles per second; we have learned that the moon, which is some 240,000 miles from the earth, takes 27 days to make one revolution; and, we are told that a tortoise may live to be about 100 years, while some flies live only for one day. Some of the watches that we use to measure time are so sophisticated that they have their own vocabulary to explain how they are used. There are stop watches that can record time to the nearest fifth, tenth, or hundredth of a second, and there are cameras that can capture time up to a millisecond, or a thousandth of a second, which is fast enough to create a stop motion effect. Some time measurements are so small that they require a computer to sort them out. For example, for the personal computer to execute a single software command, it may take only two to four nanoseconds, which are billionths of a second. Today we even have atomic clocks, which are so staggeringly accurate that they will neither lose nor gain more than a second in 3 million years. On the atomic level, a second is defined as the duration of 9,192,361,770 cycles of radiation corresponding to the transition between two energy levels of the Cesium atom.

So, we have come a long way in learning how to measure time, but the practical and personal question is, "what do we do with the time we have?" Time keeps moving on, and we cannot stop it. Time is precious, and each day is a new gift given to us by the Almighty, who created it. Yesterday is gone, and tomorrow is not here yet, so all we have is the present. But, if we use the present according to God's plan, we will accumulate memories that will rise up and bless us. Not only that, but each day lived with integrity will prepare us for the new challenges that we will face tomorrow.

Nathaniel Hawthorne once said, "Time flies over us, but leaves its shadow behind." We often hear people take about "killing Time!" What a tragedy it is to kill time; it is too precious to murder. We need to use it wisely.

Will Rogers said, "I never yet talked to a man who wanted to save time who could tell me what he was going to do with the time he saved." Today is a blessed gift from God, and it is good if we use it wisely. We can shout in agreement with Ralph Waldo Emerson who said, "this time, like all times, is a very good one, if we but know what to do with it."

Reading from the New Testament, using the Wilton Translation, let's see what James 1:1-27 has to say about how we should use our time:

"*(1) James, a slave of God and of the Lord Jesus Christ, sends greetings to the twelve tribes of the dispersion.*

"*(2) Count it all joy, my brothers, when your are involved in various trials, (3) for you know that the testing of your faith produces steadfastness. (4) And let steadfastness finish its work, so that you may be perfect and complete, lacking in nothing. (5) If anyone of you lacks wisdom, let him ask God, who gives to all generously and without insulting, and it will be given to him. (6) But he must ask in faith, never doubting; for the doubting person is like a wave of the sea that is driven and tossed by the wind. (7) That person should not think that he would receive anything from the Lord, (8) for he is double-minded and unsettled in all his ways.*

"*(9) Let the brother in his humble circumstances boast in his exaltation, (10) and the rich man in his humiliation, because he is like a flower that will soon pass away. (11) For the sun rises with the scorching wind and dries up the plant, and the petals fall off and the beauty of its appearance is destroyed; so also the rich man in the pursuit of his business will fade away.*

"*(12) Blessed is the man who remains steadfast under trial, because when he is approved, he will receive the crown of life that God has promised to those who love him. (13) Let no man say when he is tempted, "I am being tempted by God." For God cannot be tempted with evil, and he does not himself tempt anyone. (14) For each person is tempted by his own passions when he is allured and enticed by them. (15) Then lust, being conceived, gives birth to sin, and sin, when it has reached maturity, brings forth death.*

"(16) My dear brothers do not be led astray. (17) Every good giving and every perfect gift comes down from above from the Father of lights, with whom there is no variation, or a shadow cast by turning. (18) Of his will he brought us forth through the word of truth that we should be a kind of first fruits of his creatures.

"(19) Know this my dear brothers. Every man must be quick to hear, slow to speak, and slow to anger; (20) for the wrath of man does not work the righteousness of God. (21) Therefore put away all filthiness and every vicious excess, and in meekness receive the implanted word, which is able to save your souls.

"(22) Be doers of the word and not only hearers of the word, deceiving yourselves. (23) For if anyone is a hearer of the word and not a doer, he is like a man looking at his natural face in a mirror; (24) for he sees himself but he goes away, and immediately he forgets what he looked like.

(25) But the person who looks in the perfect law of freedom, and continues to do so, not being a hearer who forgets, but a doer of works—that person will be blessed in what he does.

"(26) If anyone thinks he is religious but does not bridle his tongue, but deceives his own heart, his religion is worthless. (27) Religion that is pure and stainless before God is this, to visit the orphans and widows in their affliction, and to keep oneself unstained by the world."

Now, let us examine what it says in this first chapter of James. James begins by saying that he is a slave of God and of the Lord Jesus Christ. He uses the word, δοῦλος (doulos), meaning "slave," but which is sometimes translated as "servant." The actual Greek word for "servant" is διάκονος (diakonos). It is interesting that the word, διάκονος (diakonos), is translated in the KJV by the Latin word, "minister," 29 times, by a French word, "servant," 7 times, and by a transliteration of this Greek word, as "deacon," 3 times. James, as does Paul, considers himself a "slave" of Jesus. Slavery has caused many problems in the world, and we shun from the sound of the word. However, since Jesus is the perfect master, it is a wonderful relationship to be His slave. It is like the imputed righteousness that He endows us with, which is really the only righteousness that we have. His imputed righteousness far exceeds the law. It is that silent voice that tells us what to do. Jesus never leads us wrong, and he always tells us the best way for us to go.

James 1:2-3 tells us that we are to count our trials as joy when they come. You can be assured that they will be coming, and it is not a matter of "if," but "when," they arrive. When they come, we are to respond in faith. The Greek word that expresses this is πίστις (pistis), which means, "faith, trust, faithfulness, belief, conviction, or doctrine." It is used 243 times in the New Testament. The testing of our faith produces steadfastness, but we must stand firm, because if we are doubting, we are like the instability of the sea. When steadfastness is finished, we may be perfect and complete, lacking in nothing. If we lack wisdom, we can ask for it, and He will give it to us.

We do not know ahead of time the details of the trials to come. We are all at different levels in our personal lives. There are many areas of temptation, and our age is laden with significant temptations. Some of the temptations that we might list are sexual perversion, hostility, drugs, liquor, depression, or self-seeking ambition. Whatever the trial, if we respond rightly, it can be a steppingstone to a more mature lifestyle.

How do we handle it when times are evil or when things go wrong? We should never blame it on God, because He is always interested in giving us the best in life. Remember that there are always divine ways to respond to the problems of life. For instance, in regard to the temptation of perverted sex, we can respond with purity of thought and action; to sensuality, the answer is the discipline of godly behavior; to idolatry, the way of integrity is a commitment to the one true God; to drugs, the response is to flee from their presence. If we should be slandered by a neighbor, the appropriate response is not to say equally degrading things in return, but to remember that the Bible says, "Vengeance belongs to God." When we submit to Got, there is always a way to respond by good rather than by evil.

Even though the times are evil, we can redeem the time and bring good out of it. All through the history of mankind, evil things have happened in each generation. However, there have been people in every generation who have brought good in the midst of evil.

When Paul wrote to the Romans, he emphasized that the gospel was the power of salvation to all who believe. He said that it is the righteousness of God that has been revealed from faith to faith. In speaking about faith, Paul also quoted from Habakkuk, which emphasizes that "the righteous will live by faith" (Roman 1:17; Galatians 3:11; Hebrews 10:38). If we look more thoroughly at the passage from Habakkuk, we find that Habakkuk was pleading with God for Him to explain what was happening in his day. In Habakkuk 1:3, he asked, "Why do you make me look at injustice? Why do you tolerate wrong?" The Lord responded in verse 1:6 saying, "I am raising up the Babylonians, that ruthless and impetuous people, who sweep across the whole earth to seize dwelling places not their own."

In a second complaint, Habakkuk asks in verse 1:13, "Why are you silent while the wicked swallow up those more righteous than themselves." And, in verses 2:4-5, the Lord replied, "See, he is puffed up; his desires are not upright—but the righteous will live by his faith—indeed, wine betrays him; he is arrogant and never at rest. Because he is as greedy as the grave and like death is never satisfied, he gathers to himself all the nations and takes captive all the peoples." After the end of this discourse, seeing that God was still in control, Habakkuk was content in saying, "I will wait patiently for the day of calamity to come on the nation invading us."

In the Romans 1:17 passage, Paul was saying that the gospel is a life of faith, and it is not our prerogative to question the God of the Universe. Regardless of the situation, we are to live by faith. Some evil people may have temporal power over nations and peoples; some rich people may, with greed, sweep up the wealth of the poor; some depraved people with perverted minds may exploit the virtues of the simple. Although the times are evil and sin is evident, God is on His throne; evil is ultimately punished, and righteousness exalts any nation. God never gets in a hurry, but He is always on time.

We see many things that are evil and not good. Yes, the times are evil, but we do not need to surrender to them. We need to make the best of the situation before us. We never tell God what to do, and neither do we question His actions. He knows what the sins of the people are. He has the power and ability to do what needs to be done.

So, how do we redeem the time? His will must become our will. Our prayers are to find his will, and our works must be to carry out the details of His direction. Then, we can be a part of his redemptive plan for the world. In His plan we always respond to good or evil by good, never by evil. If we are in doubt, then we can ask for wisdom, and He will give it to us. It is not necessary for me to know His plans for the future; I only need to know what He has for me to do today!

This is our challenge—to redeem the times. If we respond today in a godly way, tomorrow it will be easier to live a holy life. Peter has words of wisdom for us to heed. In 2 Peter 3:17-18, he says, "Therefore, dear friends, since you have been forewarned, be on guard lest you are led astray by lawless men and lose your own stability. But grow in grace and knowledge of our Lord and Savior Jesus Christ. To him be the glory both now and unto the eternal day."

Repentance

Repentance is a very important word in the New Testament. It was the theme of John the Baptist as he went up and down the wilderness of Judea preaching the message of salvation. It was the message of Jesus as he began His ministry. Jesus sent The Twelve out to preach, and their message was that the people must repent. That message was then, and is now, that we must either repent or perish (Luke 13:5).

To get a full grasp of the word, "Repentance," let us examine several Greek words used in the New Testament to convey its meaning. First, let's look at the Greek verb, μετανοέω (metanoeo), which means, "to perceive afterwards." The first half of the word, μετά, means "after," implying change. The second half of the word, νοέω, means "to perceive," implying involvement with the mind or seat of moral reflection. The parts taken together mean a complete change of mind and heart away from sin, and toward God. This word is used in the NT 34 times, and it is always translated, "repent."

Another Greek word, the noun, μετάνοια (metanoia), having the same root as our first word, means, "after-thought, change of mind, repentance." It is used in the NT 24, and it is always translated, "repentance."

A third Greek word, the verb, μεταμέλομαι (metamelomai), means "regret." It has the idea of being sorry or having regret, but it does not have the idea of a change in attitude. It is found 6 times in the NT, and most translations, except for the KJV, which translates it as "repent," translate the word as "regret," or some other word with that idea. An example of the KJV usage of this word is found in Matthew 27:3, where we read that Judas "repented" and went out and hanged himself. It seems to me that "regret" would be a more accurate translation of this word.

Looking at the English definitions for the words, "repent," and "regret," there is a clear distinction in the meanings for the two words. The dictionary definition of *"repent"* [ME>OF repentir>re+pentir, to be sorry>paenitere] is,

> *"1. to turn from sin and dedicate oneself to the amendment of one's life... 2a. to feel regret or contrition... 2b. to change one's mind...."*

The dictionary definition of *"regret"* [ME regretten>MF regreter>OF re+greter, to lament, perh. Of Gmc origin: akin to ON grata, to weep] is,

> *"1a. to mourn the loss or death of... 1b. to be very sorry for (as to one's mistakes)...."*

The word, "repentance," is so important to the Christian message that we must have a deep comprehension of its meaning. Let us first look at what it is not, and, then, we will look at what it is. Concerning the church, it means more than just membership.

The institutional church is a wonderful organization, but the local church was never established to save individuals. Only God can save the souls of individuals, and it must be one by one. It cannot be done by humans. Adding a name to the roll of a church is not sufficient. Some of the most evil people in the world have been members of some local church. Even Judas was chosen by Jesus to be one of His apostles, but his heart was never right, because he was a devil from the beginning. There are many denominations and kinds of churches today, but none have the power of salvation. Church membership without repentance is of no value.

Jesus gave us rituals to observe in our worship services. They are very important to observe, because they have great teaching value. For example, baptism is a ritual that teaches the essentials of the new birth in Christ, but it has no efficacious power to make one holy. It only portrays something that has already happened. It portrays a beautiful symbolism of one's death to sin and the resurrection of life from the grave, of leaving the old life to walk in the newness of life in Christ. But, if the experience of the new birth has not taken place, this baptism has no meaning, because the water alone does not have power to wash away sins.

The Lord's Supper is another beautiful ritual of the church. It is a testimony to the world that we have a new covenant with our Lord and that we have spiritual bread for daily consumption. The ritual is done in remembrance of Jesus, but the physical bread has no power to change a life of sin or to live a life of holiness.

Repentance is more than doing good deeds or works of salvation. In Ephesians 2:1-10, Paul reminded the Ephesians that they had lived in the lusts of the flesh and were by nature children of wrath, but that "God who is rich in mercy, because of the great love by which he loved us, and when we were dead in trespasses he made us alive in Christ Jesus—by grace are you saved—and raised us up and seated us in the heavenlies with Christ Jesus." In other words, we are not saved by works or by keeping the law. We are only saved by grace through faith, and this is the gift of God. We are His work of art, created in Christ Jesus for good works.

We are also not saved through emotionalism. We are not saved by feelings, because it takes more than emotionalism to regenerate a heart of evil and to make it a heart of purity. For example, people often get emotional at ball games, but this is so temporary. If at the next game their favorite team loses, those once exuberant emotions may turn into grief and depression. Likewise, people may have an emotional experience at church, but they may then walk away with the same old sins, the same filthy habits, the same prejudices, the same grudges, the same indulgences, the same hostilities, and the same lifestyle. That is not repentance. That is only emotionalism. Salvation, with true repentance, means a new lifestyle.

Repentance is a transition of personality and, with the change of heart, the means of salvation. Since we have all sinned, we all need to repent. In Romans 3:23, we are told that we all have sinned and come short of the glory of God. That means that because we have all sinned, we are alienated from God, because Sin alienates us from God. Remember the prodigal son, how his rebellion put him in a filthy pigpen. His condition reminds us that just as he could not have fellowship with his father in that filthy lifestyle, we also cannot have fellowship with our Holy Father while we are still actively in our filthy lifestyles. At one point, the Prodigal realized his state, and he left the pigpen and turned and went back to his father's house. That was repentance.

There are two paths to follow in life. One path is the natural way of the flesh, and the other path is the life of repentance. When abiding in the lifestyle of the works of the flesh, the dominant desires of the flesh become the controlling master of the individual. The life of repentance is another, opposing, lifestyle. After an initial time of repentance, when we accept Jesus as our Lord and Savior, we begin to grow in knowledge and spirit, where there is always a higher level to achieve. Therefore, we keep repenting, leaving the status quo, and moving up the ladder to become more like Jesus. As we grow in grace, we become aware of more of the ugly motives in our lives, and we continue to repent and grasp for more Christ-like motives.

The way of the transgressor is hard, but the way of the righteous is a light that dawns to a new day. Those who follow Satan have hard times. Witness the fornicator, who forsakes his family to seek after another woman to satisfy his fleshly desires; witness the drug addict, who gives her/his body to please the desires of the flesh; witness the glutton, who lives to abuse his/her body with excessive desire for food and drink; witness the drunkard, who lives only for another drink; witness the prostitute, who sells her body for the pleasures of life. On the other hand, witness the godly person, who loves his family and is respected and loved by them; witness the faithful disciple of Jesus, who lives by faith and enjoys every day of it; witness the Christian, who lives through many difficulties but can see that all things work together for good to those who are called of God.

Jesus taught that the only way to salvation is through repentance. In Luke 13:4-5, Jesus mentioned about the awful fate of the 18 people who were killed when the tower of Siloam fell on them. The thought going around was that those people killed by the falling tower must have been very sinful to have experienced such a terrible fate. But, Jesus said, "…unless you repent you will all likewise perish."

True repentance is a changing of the personality. In 2 Corinthians 5:17-18, Paul tells us what happens with true repentance, saying, "Therefore if anyone is in Christ, he is a new creation; the old has passed away, behold, the new has come! All this is from God, who through Christ has reconciled us to himself and has given us the ministry of reconciliation." The result is a new person and new lifestyle. It is a change from rebellion to acceptance and fellowship.

After the change of lifestyle that has come because of repentance, our loyalty has been changed. Previously, we had been slaves of sin, but now we become slaves of righteousness. Romans 6:19-23 says,

> ***"(19) ...For as you offered the members of your body as slaves of uncleanness and to iniquity unto iniquity, so now offer the members of your bodies to righteousness for sanctification. (20) For when you were slaves of sin, you were free in regards to righteousness. (21) Therefore, what harvest were you then reaping, from the things which now make you blush? For the end of those things is death. (22) But now, having been freed from sin and enslaved to God, your harvest is sanctification, and the end eternal life. (23) For the wages of sin is death, but the gift of God is eternal life in Christ Jesus our Lord."***

This new life prepares us for the proclamation of the Good News of Jesus the King of Kings. His Kingdom has arrived. When we become a part of this new kingdom, it becomes a part of our responsibility to tell others about the good news of salvation. The Kingdom of God is a present reality. The Messiah has arrived. It is not political, but spiritual. It is not national, but universal. We read in 2 Peter 3:9, "The Lord is not slow concerning his promise as some understand slowness, but is long-suffering toward you, and it is not his will for anyone to perish, but for all to come to repentance."

When Paul, as a young executive of the Jewish Sanhedrin, went to Damascus to destroy the Christian Church, he was a self-righteous Pharisee who thought that he was doing the will of God. But, when Jesus met him on his way, he became aware of his sinfulness and repented of his evil ways. Paul repented, and instead of hunting the Christians to persecute them, he sought after them to love them and to work with them. This experience began a lifetime of repentance. In his closing years, he wrote to the Philippians (3:12-14) telling them about his intensive desire to be more like Jesus, saying "It is not that I have already attained to this, or that I have become perfect, but I press on that I may take hold of it, but this one thing I do: forgetting the things that are behind, I am stretching forward to what lies ahead. My eyes are on the goal and I am pressing on for the high calling of God in Christ Jesus."

Saved
(Ephesians 2:1-10)

Ephesus was the important city of commerce in Asia Minor in the days of Paul. It was the crossroad for the people going from the East, or West, or North, to the South. It had the large pagan temple of Artemis (Diana, in Latin), one of the seven wonders of the ancient world. Also, in Corinth there was the temple of Aphrodite. Both of these temples were places of unholy prostitution. They exemplified the works of the flesh.

Paul reminds the Christians of Ephesus of where they had been in relation to sin and how they had been delivered from their sins. They had been living in the lusts of the flesh and of the mind. In Paul's letter to the Galatians (5:19-21), he names the works of the flesh as "fornication, uncleanness, sensuality, idolatry, abuse of drugs, hostility, fits of rage, self-seeking ambition, dissention, factions, envy, drunkenness, carousing, and the like."

Ephesians 2:1-10 gives us a dramatic picture of the devastation of sin. It not only tells us about the condition of the people in the day of Paul, but it is a commentary of the natural man of today.

In Ephesians 2:1-3, Paul wrote,

"(1) You were dead in your trespasses and sins, (2) when you followed the evil ways of the present age, according to the ruler...of the air, which is now operating in the sons of disobedience, (3) among whom we also conducted ourselves then in the lusts of the flesh and the mind, and were by nature children of wrath, as the rest."

They were dead; they were alienated from the source of life. The cause of alienation and death was sin. In their moral decay, they were totally indifferent to the things of God. In this depravity, they were in a quagmire of iniquity, without hope in this world and in the world to come. They were enslaved in the manner of their walking; they were living in the atmosphere of evil desires; they were following the dictates of Satan.

In their desperation, they received a wonderful message from the Eternal. Paul declares (Ephesians 2:4-7),

"(4) But God, who is rich in mercy, because of the great love by which he loved us, (5) and when we were dead in the trespasses, made us alive in Christ Jesus—by grace you are saved— (6) and raised us up and seated us in the heavenlies with Christ Jesus, (7) in order that in the coming ages he might show the exceeding riches of his grace in kindness toward us in Christ Jesus."

God's grace is a refiner's fire. Those who were dead were made alive in righteousness; those who were blinded and enslaved by Satan were enlightened and became free to become qualified to carry the message of salvation and life; they had been elevated from the cesspool of evil to sit with Christ in heavenly places.

Salvation was a matter of grace, but it is received through faith. It was then, and is now, available to all who by faith will receive it.

Paul explains the new lifestyle in relation to works. He wrote (Ephesians 2:8-10),

"(8) For you have been saved by grace through faith; and this is not from you, it is

the gift of God— (9) not of works, lest anyone should boast. (10) For we are his work of art, created in Christ Jesus for good works, which God had previously prepared, that we should walk in them."

We are not to work for salvation, but, after we are saved by grace, we become God's servants to share his gospel with those who desperately need it.

After we have been delivered from the works of the flesh, we can pursue a life of meaningful relationships. This new mode of life is well expressed by Augustus M. Toplady (1740-1778) in his hymn, "Rock of Ages, Cleft for me." The words of this song say,

"Rock of Ages, Cleft for me, Let me hide myself in Thee;
Let the water and the blood, From Thy wounded side which flowed,
Be of sin the double cure, Save from wrath and make me pure."

We must have double cure, which involves both the forgiveness of our sins and a new lifestyle of purity.

Let us now look at our text in Ephesians from 3 different vantage points. First, let us realize what we have been saved **from**. We are saved from an evil thought pattern—the desires of the mind and flesh, or to put it another way, we are delivered from the works of the flesh. Secondly, we will look at it in relation to what we have been saved **to**. Thirdly, we will seek to find what we have been saved **for**.

Please note that the sin of fornication heads the list of the works of the flesh that we have been saved **from**. It is sexual perversion in all its forms. It is taking something precious and beautiful and adulterating it—like putting slop in your dinner plate! God made man and woman in his likeness, but physically, he made them different: male and female. The two were to become one in flesh, and that oneness was to be consummated in the marriage bed. And it was through this holy union that was the means of propagating new life. It is the most sacred relationship between human individuals. It was never meant to be a toy or plaything, but it was meant to be an expression of eternal love between the husband and wife. When it is used outside of that context, it heads the list of the works of the flesh.

The wrong use of sex has been the downfall of many. Witness the strongman Samson, who lost his way when he was tempted to visit Delilah, the prostitute; witness David, the king, when he looked over the curtains to see Bathsheba bathing; witness Solomon, the wise man, who took hundreds of wives for his fleshly desires and for political power. In the case of Samson, it led to blindness and suicide; in the case of David, it led to a curse that was upon his family, and 4 of his children were killed; in the case of Solomon, his irresponsibility caused the split of the kingdom.

We, the ones here at Emmanuel Baptist Church, are more likely to be guilty of hostility than of fornication. It is easy to hold grudges and ill will against those who may have not treated us as we think they should. It may be that we do not like that person who does things better then we do. It may be that we do not like that person who is more handsome or beautiful than we are. Or, it may be that we do not like people who are of another color, another living standard, another social status, or another race.

It is easy for us to be hostile to other people. We must notice that hostility is classified among the works of the flesh. Our job is to win the world for Christ. We cannot do that if we harbor hostility. The true gospel must be delivered with love and compassion.

What, then, are we saved *to*? How is the new life to be compared with the old life? Paul says, "If anyone be in Christ, he is a new creation; the old things passed away, the new has come!" The old works of the flesh have disappeared, and now we can enjoy the fruit of the Spirit, which is "love, joy, peace, long-suffering, kindness, goodness, faithfulness, meekness, and self-control." We can now love instead of hate; we can have joy instead of worry; we can have peace instead of fighting; we can have patience instead of contention; we can have kindness instead of rudeness; we can have faithfulness instead of sinfulness; we can have meekness instead of self-righteousness; we can have self-control instead of rebellion.

We do not have to live in defeat. We are God's children; we are the salt of the earth; we are the lights of the world. We can now sit with Christ in heavenly places; we can forgive others, regardless of what they have done; we can love others, regardless as to how they treat us; we can live in faith each day that the Lord gives us. We can have redemptive talk and a good word to exchange with others.

Finally, we are saved *for* good works. We do not do good works to be saved; we do good works, because we have become children of God, and that is now our nature. As Paul says in Ephesians 2:10, "For we are his work of art, created in Christ Jesus for good works, which God had previously prepared, that we should walk in them." We are a product of his making. This is expressed in the Greek word, ποίημα (poiema), which is the word for "poem." We are no longer prose; we are poems created for good works.

When He endows us with salvation, he gives us the tools for our work of evangelism. We have been reconciled to him; so, we have the ministry of reconciliation. As we saw in Ephesians 2:4-7, our lives are to reflect God's grace and to show others what salvation means.

We have become the dwelling place for the Almighty. To be in Christ means that He has come to dwell within us. The Spirit can lead us into paths of righteousness.

Where are you today? If you should be in the cesspool of evil thoughts, talking about evil, walking in the ways of the unrighteousness of sin, God's grace can save you and give you the blessings of eternal life. Now is the day of salvation. The choice to reject the call leads to death; the choice to accept this great salvation brings eternal life. You make the call!

The Attitude of Gratitude

It is very important to have the right attitude about life. According to longtime friend, Dr. Barker, "You cannot have a good day with a bad attitude; and, you cannot have a bad day with a good attitude."

So, the good life is not determined by one's education, or wealth, or racial extraction, or power, or health, or status. It can be the challenge and the victory of the poor, the weak, the sick, or the "unimportant."

The word, "*attitude*," is from the French, which is also from Late Latin, meaning, "aptitude," or "fitness." It is a mental position or a feeling of emotions with regards to a fact or state.

The word, "*gratitude*," comes from Middle English, which comes from Latin, meaning, "gratus," or "grateful." Gratitude is the state of being grateful or having thankfulness.

Our text, which is from Philippians 4:4-13, says, *"(4) Rejoice in the Lord always. I will say it again: rejoice! (5) Let your patient steadfastness be evident to everyone. The Lord is near. (6) Do not worry about anything, but in everything, by prayer and petition with thanksgiving, let your requests be known to God. (7) And the peace of God that transcends all our dreams will guard your hearts and your thoughts in Christ Jesus.*

"(8) Finally, brothers, whatever is true, whatever is noble, whatever is pure, whatever is lovely, whatever is praiseworthy, yes, on moral excellence and

praise—let your thoughts dwell. (9)
Practice the things you learned, and
received, and heard, and saw in me, and
the God of peace will be with you.

"(10) I rejoiced greatly in the Lord
that your concern for me has been renewed;
but indeed you have been concerned for
me, but you had no opportunity to show it.
(11) I do not say this because I am in need,
for I have learned to be self-sufficient
regardless of the circumstances. (12) I
know what it is to be humbled and I know
how it is to abound. I have learned the
secret of how to respond in every
situation—to be filled or to be hungry, to
have plenty or to be in need. (13) I can do
all things through him who strengthens
me."

This idea of living in the spirit of rejoicing, joyfulness, and thankfulness is emphasized very much in the Bible. It is interesting to note that joy and grace come from the same root. They are companion words; if you have grace you have joy; and, you cannot have real joy without the grace of God.

The attitude of hostility is the opposite of the attitude of gratitude. This is ingratitude, rebellion, rudeness, insolence, and harshness. It is the attitude of saying that "everyone is out to get me."

Rebellion begins with an attitude toward God and His righteousness; and, rebellion leads to a life of arrogance and hostility. The common companion of the word is "bitterness." Hostility and bitterness is the picture of a destitute life.

The attitude of bitterness and rebelliousness never lets one live in the present. Life becomes miserable, but in the mind of the bitter and the rebellious, it is because of the past. Someone stands out in his/her mind who was the culprit. He/she is the one to blame for all those troublesome problems. So, it festers in the mind, and it becomes an obsession never to leave—living rent-free! "That was the cause of my torment," one thinks, whether a drinking habit, or using drugs, or a woman/man chaser. There is no place for forgiveness or a time to forget. So, because of faulty thinking, the good life is destroyed, and others are devastated.

To the rebellious, the past is a nightmare; the present is a carnal existence; the future is an awful nightmare come true. We do not need to go to other parts of the world or to go back in time to find examples, because these people are here with us, even today. In fact, some may be here, now, in this place, and at this time. They are the people who live in the negative, rather than the positive; their experience is the bitterness of soul, rather than the sweetness of grace; it is the shadow of the rocky past, rather than the sunshine of God's grace in the present; it is the darkness of despair, rather than the hope of the future; it is the frown of hatred, rather than the smile of forgiveness.

Our attitudes determine our actions, whether to live selfishly or to be ready to lend a helping hand to one who needs it. Some people operate on the philosophy of "**what is yours is mine, if I can get it.**" Many scams are operated on this principle. The story of the Good Samaritan well illustrates this attitude of life.

In this story of the Good Samaritan, there was a traveler going from Jerusalem to Jericho. Some thieves robbed him of his property, and in the process of their rough treatment, they almost killed him, leaving him wounded and dying alongside the road. They were not concerned with the welfare of the other person. They were only interested in what he had, rather than his personal interests. They were concerned about getting his property; and they were content to leave him dying by the roadside away from his loved ones.

As the man lay dying, a priest and a Levite came by on the other side of the road. Their philosophy was "*what I have is mine, and I plan to keep it.*" They had no interest in getting involved with the dying man. Their excuse was that since they did not cause his trouble, why should they go out of the way to help him? Since his business was not their business, they were content in tending to their own business and letting him tend to his. So, they left a man dying, with no hope of recovery.

But, praise the Lord, there are some people who have the attitude of "*what is mine is yours, if you need it*"! That was the attitude of the Samaritan who was traveling from Jerusalem to Jericho and beyond. Evidently, he was going on a business trip, but because of his heart of compassion for the wounded man, he crossed over to the wounded man's side of the road to help him.

The three attitudes of life mentioned are further illustrated by the story of the Prodigal Son. When the Prodigal left home, he went with the attitude of "*what is mine is mine, and I want it now!*" So, he demanded for his father to give him his inheritance, immediately. This was from a selfishness that had no concern for the father or for the brother.

The elder brother had the attitude of "*what is mine is mine, and I am going to keep it.*" So, when his "no good" rebellious brother later returned to home, he did not want to help him. The Father tried to plead with the elder son by saying of the younger brother, "this brother of yours was dead, but now he lives," but the elder brother had no intentions of helping his brother. His attitude was that "he made his own bed, so let him sleep on it. He made a fool of himself, so why should I help him!" In fact, he did not want to acknowledge that he was a brother, because he referred to him only as "this son of yours." He wanted no part of the Father's celebration that the Prodigal had come home.

The Father's attitude is the one we ought to try to emulate. His attitude was "**what is mine is yours, if you need it.**" So, the Father gives grace to all who will receive it on His terms. With that attitude, the Prodigal was forgiven, and he was encouraged to live a good life.

Looking back at our scripture text, in Philippians 4:4, Paul says, "Rejoice in the Lord always." It is a constant frame of the mind, which is always seeing the blessings of life and rejoicing in them. The scripture also tells us to "not worry about anything, but in everything, by prayer and petition with thanksgiving, let your requests be known to God. And the peace of God that transcends all our dreams will guard your hearts and your thoughts in Christ Jesus" (Philippians 4:6-7). Then, Paul gives a list of things that we ought to think about. His list includes whatever is true, noble, pure, lovely, praiseworthy, and of moral excellence. These are things on which to let your thoughts dwell. When we have done this, we can be assured that the God of peace will be with us (Philippians 4:8-9).

Paul goes on to say, "I have learned the **secret** of how to live in every situation—to be filled or to be hungry, to have plenty or to be in need." The word for "secret" in this quotation comes from the Greek verb, μυέω (mueo). Both the verb and the noun, μυστήριον (musterion), come from the same root. The Greek noun, μυστήριον, is used 27 times in the N.T. In the Greco-Roman world, the use of this word was what was called a "religious technical." It referred to a religious secret that was confided only to the initiated, but that is not the sense in which it is used in the N.T. In the N.T., the word refers to that which can only be known through revelation, mediated from God, and what was known before. We get the English word, "mystery," from this word, but it has a different meaning. In our use of the English word, the mystery is still a secret. In Greek, it is no longer a secret, because, by God's revelation, we now understand it; it is no longer unknown.

The verb, μυέω, found in our text in Philippians 4:12, is used only once in the Bible. This is another "religious technical" term, which generally means, "to initiate into sacred mystery religions, or to initiate or instruct." In the N.T., it is used figuratively. The word used in this reference is in the perfect tense, and in the passive voice, which means that we have been initiated and we have learned the secret. We have been instructed how to do something. The secret here has come by the revelation of God, by His grace, which gives victory in all circumstances.

Paul had been in many hardships. But, he had learned the secret of how to respond in every situation. When we have been initiated into His grace, we have the secret of how to respond to all of life's circumstances.

In the March 14 reading of My Utmost of His Highest, Oswald Chambers has two profound statements. One says, "If a child gives in to selfishness, he will find it to be the most enslaving tyranny on the earth." The other statement is, "But yielding to Jesus will break every kind of slavery in any person's life." Thus, Chambers introduces us to a terrible attitude, but, on the other hand, he gives us the cure.

So, what is your attitude toward life? If it is a bad attitude, it can be changed to a good attitude, by the grace of God. It can change the gambler, the fornicator, the drug addict, the elder brother attitude, the attitude of hostility, or any slavery of the works of the flesh. It can change hatred to love; the gambler to honesty; the sexually perverse to purity of thought; hostility to compassion; defeat to victory; dissension to peace; from hell to heaven. If you will only deny yourself and surrender your life to Jesus, you can be initiated into a life of holiness, which gives you the secret of how to respond to all of life's experiences. Now is the day of salvation. Come, before it is too late, and rejoice, by God's grace, in the Attitude of Gratitude.

The Crown of Righteousness

Precious in the sight of the Lord is the death of his saints.
(Psalm 116:15)

Another year is just about gone. Time just keeps moving on. Christmas came and went one more time. We are one year nearer to the grave than this time last year, and I trust that the year has made us better men and women.

It was about this time of the year, on December 29, 1948, that I heard the testimony of a great saint of God. At that time, he was about to go home to be with his Lord, and the Almighty had appeared to him in such a real way, that he asked me to tell his experience to the church. And, this I did. His experience has so been impressed upon my mind that I have told it to the church every year about this time. As of 2008, sixty years have passed since that day in 1948, and since I have now been in Bryan for 41 years, I have told it to Emmanuel Baptist Church at least 41 times. To me, it does not get old, and I trust it does not to you.

Shortly after I moved on the church field at Bellevue, Texas, a great saint of God, Rev. W.H. Neeley, a minister of the gospel for more than half a century, at the age of 92, passed from the world of the here and now to the world of eternity. This was on the afternoon of December 29, 1948. The next day, I had charge of his funeral. His life touched mine only for a few days, but the influence and encouragement and inspiration that I received from him will always be a part of my life.

As Bro. Neeley was having this wonderful experience with the Lord, he did not think he would get back to church, so that was why he asked me to share his "eternal experience" with the church. On that day it was cold, rainy, and sloppy when I went to his home. Uncle Ben Davis had been there before me, and as he was leaving, he met me at the door. He told me that "the old man" was saying strange things. When I entered the house, I sat down in the living room with Bro. Neeley and his wife and his brother-in-law and wife. As we hovered around the wood burning stove in the middle of the room, he asked me to read the 116th Psalm. As I read and came to the 15th verse, where it says "Precious in the sight of the Lord is the death of his saints," Bro. Neeley shouted out a praise to the Lord. Then, he said that the Lord was so near to him that he could almost touch the hem of his garment. At that moment, he was living in a state of ecstasy.

The best description of the event came from his brother-in-law, who later, during the funeral elegy, said, "The Scripture, 'I know in whom I have believed and am persuaded he is able to keep me until that day' was a fitting part of your life. That day came on Christmas morning. For several hours, it seemed that you were in a coma. When you awakened, it seemed you had passed into that new life in which all former things had passed away, and you stood glorified in the presence of God. From that time, you seemed to be present with God and in love with everybody. 'Twas then you silently slipped into the silent halls of death."

At the time of his passing, as far as I could tell, Bro. Neeley was the happiest person that I had ever seen. He rejoiced in the presence of death. It was almost noontime when I arrived, and later that afternoon, he passed away. There was no indication of any sickness, or pain, or even a bad cold. The time had come for him to receive his crown of righteousness. So, he left with a shout of glory.

The old year is about gone, and the new year is about here. How many more earth years do we have? No one knows, but one thing that we do know, each year we are getting a little older, and, for certain, one day we will meet death. In all of the joys and burdens of this present world, may we never loose sight of the true purpose of life! It is wise and good for young people to save and prepare for old age, but, even so, it is more important that we prepare for eternity.

When we come to the end of this earthly pilgrimage, many things that we thought to be important will fade into insignificance; and, many things that we neglected to do will become to us intensely important. Then will be the time that most of us will look at life and see it in its true perspective. Some may look back on life and say that they have had a good time, or that they became popular and well-known, or that they made a fortune, or that they accomplished many things. The drunkard may want one more drink; the gambler may want to shuffle the cards once more; the gossiper may want to spread another ugly rumor; the libertine may want to wallow in the lust of the flesh once again. But, the godly saint may want to bless his family once more; the gospel preacher may want to preach one more sermon; the prayer warrior may want to intercede for his friend; the good neighbor may want to help his friend one more time. When most of us come to die, we will be humble and prayerful with a repentant heart.

You may recall in the Bible of the story of the seer Balaam, who taught King Balak to cast "a stumbling block before the children of Israel, to eat things sacrificed unto idols, and commit fornication." But when Balaam came to die, when he saw that his physical life was about to be terminated, he said, "Let me die the death of the righteous, and let my last end be like his!" This is the cry of many people at the end of this life's journey. They want to indulge in the lust of the flesh in this life, but then live with the people of God in eternity.

Some men of faith have been able to paint beautiful pictures of death and immortality. William Jennings Bryan said, "If this invisible germ of life in the grain of wheat can thus pass unimpaired through 3,000 resurrections, I shall not doubt that my soul has power to clothe itself with a new body, suited to its new existence, when this earthly frame has crumbled into dust."

Stephen, of the New Testament, was the first Christian martyr. He was stoned to death. His last words were, "Behold, I see the heavens opened, and the Son of man standing at the right hand of God. Lord Jesus, receive my spirit." Then, he knelt down and cried with a loud voice, "Lord, do not hold this sin against them." Then, "he fell asleep."

Paul also had the perception to look with great anticipation toward entering into the heavenly realm. He had been treated as a criminal here on earth, but he knew that there was a crown of righteousness laid up for him in heaven. He had been condemned by an evil judge; but, in heaven, he knew that he would be rewarded with the crown of righteousness by a righteous judge. With this thought in mind, Paul wrote to Timothy the words, "For I am already being sacrificed, and the time of my departure has come. I have fought the good fight, I have finished the course, I have kept the faith; therefore the crown of righteousness is reserved for me, which the Lord, the righteous judge, will give me in that day and not only to me but to all who have loved his appearing" (2 Timothy 4:6-8). Many since the days of Paul have also seen the heavenly vision.

When Whittier, the Quaker poet, came to die, his nurse came into his room and began to pull the shades down, but he beckoned her to raise them, instead of pulling them down. He wanted to go out in the glow and warmth of the morning light.

The last words of a saint by the name of Cookman were, "I am sweeping through the gates."

Another dying saint said, "Drive on!" He was coming to the end of the journey, and he wanted the chariot to hasten on, to bring him home.

John Wesley said, as he was dying, "The best of all is God is with me."

Just before John Huss was burned at the stake, he was given a last chance to renounce his teachings and go free, but he said, "No, I never preached any doctrine of an evil tendency; and what I taught with my lips, I now seal with my blood." As he was being burned at the stake on the charges of being a heretic, a paper miter was placed on his head, and the bishop said, "Now we commit thy soul unto the devil." John Huss, lifting his eyes up towards the heavens, said, "But I commend into thy hands, O Lord Jesus Christ, my spirit which thou hast redeemed." When the flames wrapped around him, his loud and cheerful voice could be heard singing a hymn, through all the crackling of the flames and the noise of the multitudes.

Jerome of Prague was executed at the same spot as John Huss. As he went to his execution, he sang several hymns and prayed fervently. Jerome embraced the stake with great cheerfulness. The executioner went behind him to light the fire, but this great saint of God said, "Come here and kindle it before my eyes, for if I had been afraid of it, I would not have come to this place." He sang as he died, and the last words he was heard saying were, "This soul in flames I offer, Christ, to thee."

We must always remember that we are approaching the end of the trail. Psalm 90 has wonderful advice for all of us.   In Verse 10, it says, "The days of our years are threescore years and ten (70); and if by reason of strength they be fourscore years (80), yet is their strength labor and sorrow; for it is soon cut off, and we fly away." Verse 12 says, "So teach us to number our days, that we may apply our hearts unto wisdom." Verse 17 says, "And let the beauty of the Lord our God be upon us."   That tells us that our days are soon to pass and that we should live each day to the fullest, as we pray for the beauty of the Lord to bless us.

Judgment day is approaching. We may miss some appointments in life, "but it is appointed unto men once to die," and this is one appointment we will not miss. Then, we all will realize that temporal things are insecure and perishable. We will realize that life is a stewardship and that we will be judged by it. We will realize that life is a trial in which we will be tried for an eternal verdict.

When we number our days, we will see that every thought or action has eternal consequences. We may be able to break the laws of the land and think that we are smart, but we will never successfully break the laws of God. When we try to, they break us. Every good deed will be a blessing to the giver; and, every bad deed will be a curse to the perpetrator.

Judgment day is coming. Are you ready for it? You cannot evade it! The gospel gives us a chance to embrace it. Will you accept the promise of a new life? It will prepare you for today and for eternity.

The Fruit of the Spirit
(Galatians 5:16-24)

In the fifth chapter of Galatians (5:16-24), Paul tells us about the two ways of life: one following the works of the flesh, and the other receiving the Fruit of the Spirit. One way leads to the destruction of life, and the other leads to the blessings of life. The works of the flesh indulges in satisfying the lusts of fleshly cravings; however, the Fruit of the Spirit is the result of commitment to God and his standards for a lifestyle of godly righteousness. The flesh calls out for immediate fulfillment; but, the Spirit calls out for a life of faith by grace, rather than works. The works of the flesh are self-centered, whereas, the Fruit of the Spirit is God centered.

In the first epistle of John (2:15-17), we have the admonition,

> *"(15) Do not love the world or the things in the world. If anyone loves the world, the love of the father is not in him. (16) For all that is in the world—the lust of the flesh, the lust of the eyes and the vainglory of life—does not come from the father but from the world. (17) And the world and all its allurements are passing away, but the one doing the will of God abides forever."*

The characteristics of the world are described in 3 parts: the lust of the flesh, the lust of the eyes, and the vainglory of life. The first characteristic of worldliness, the lust of the flesh, is manifested in such things as food, drink, and sex. The godly way to satisfy such desires as food and drink is to work and receive wages to buy the necessities of physical life. However, some would rather have a lifestyle of being bums, loafers, thieves, or robbers. In God's creation of male and female, it was intended that at the appropriate time, in marriage, they were to become one flesh. Through this consummation, new life is brought into existence. But, some make sex a plaything and make it filthy and destructive.

The second characteristic of worldliness, the lust of the eyes, can also be devastating. The eyes may see a new car, a beautiful home, and a luxurious wardrobe. The things lusted for may not be evil within themselves, but if there is an obsession for them without the means of obtaining them, it become the lust of the eyes. If the eye is evil, it cannot be satisfied. However, if we have a heart of gratitude, we have the ability to enjoy our blessings. If not, having a heart of unthankfulness, we are not able to enjoy the good things of life.

The third characteristic of worldliness is the vainglory of life, and it is represented by a life of boasting and arrogance. The Greek word, ἀλαλάζω (alalazo), means "to cry out loudly." It is also used as a battle cry. It is used only 2 times in the New Testament: in Mark 5:38, and in 1 Corinthians 13:1. It is bragging about one's possessions in order to impress other people.

On the other hand, the Fruit of the Spirit is treated in scripture as singular, and this fruit, καρπός (karpos), has nine attributes. The first three attributes are love, ἀγάπη (agapa), joy, χαρά (chara), and peace, εἰρήνη (eirana). One receives these gifts through the grace of God.

The next three attributes are patience, μακροθυμία (makrothumia), kindness, χραστότης (chrastotas), and goodness, ἀγαθωσύνη (agathosuna). These attributes deal with our responses to others in wholesome ways. They tell us how to respond to those in need.

The last three attributes are faithfulness, πίστις (pistis), meekness, πραΰτας (prautas), and self-control, ἐγεράτεια (egerateia). These attributes reflect the strength of character that has discipline to live a life of Christ-centered righteousness.

The lists of the works of the flesh and the Fruit of the Spirit both start with a form of love; however, one is a pseudo-love, and the other one is genuine love. Before we examine these two ways of life, we need to examine the meaning of Love.

In our English language there are different kinds of love. There is the sweetheart love, the family love, the friendship love, and the esteem love. From the dictionary, we have a definition of **Love** {(luv) n.; ME<OE lufu}:

"1. An intense affection for another person based on personal or familiar ties.
2. An expression of one's affection.
3. An intense attraction to another person based mainly on sexual desire.
4. In Mythology Eros or Cupid, was the god of love. (The representative of the god Cupid was a winged boy with a bow and arrow, used as a symbol of love.)
5. God's mercy and benevolence toward humans.
6. A zero score in tennis."

In Hebrew, the word for *love* is אָהַב (ah-hav). It is used 201 times in the Old Testament. It means "to desire, love, like, to be inflamed, to lust after." It is like our English word that can mean several kinds of love. There are several examples in scripture to show some of the uses of this word:

"Israel <u>loved</u> Joseph...." (Genesis 37:3).

"Thou shalt <u>love</u> thy neighbor...." (Leviticus 19:18).

"<u>Love</u> ye therefore the stranger...." (Deuteronomy 10:19).

"Solomon <u>loved</u> many strange women...." (1 Kings 11:1).

"Thou <u>lovest</u> evil more than good...." (Psalm 52:3).

"...all that hate me <u>love</u> death...." (Proverbs 8:36).

"Jacob <u>loved</u> Rachel...." (Genesis 29:18).

"...he (Samson) fell in <u>love</u> with a woman in the Valley of Sorek whose name as Delilah...." (Judges 16:4)—he lost his brain and his eyes in that love affair.

"...she (Gomer)...went after her <u>lovers</u>...." (Hosea 2:13).

"...the seed of Abraham my <u>friend</u>...." (Isaiah 41:8).

"...you who hate good, and <u>love</u> evil...." (Micah 3:2).

The Hebrew word for **loving-kindness** is חֶסֶד (khehsed), and it is used 232 times. It means "kindness, mercy, favor, and pity." The following are some of the ways it is used in scripture:

"...showing <u>mercy</u> to thousands...." (Exodus 20:6).

"O give thanks unto the Lord; for he is good; for his <u>mercy</u> endureth forever...." (1 Chronicles 16:34).

"...Because thy <u>loving-kindness</u> is better than life...." (Psalm 63:3).
"...For I desire <u>mercy</u>, and not sacrifice...." (Hosea 6:6).
"He hath showed thee, O man, what is good; and what doth the Lord require of thee, but to do justly, and to love <u>mercy</u>, and to walk humbly with thy God?" (Micah 6:8).

The Greeks had 4 words for Love: ἔρος (eros), στοργός (storgos), φίλος (philos), and ἀγάπη (agapa). The first attribute of the Fruit of the Spirit is ἀγάπη (agapa), which is genuine love or esteem, and without this love, all is vain. As it says in 1 Corinthians 13:1, "If I speak in the tongues of men and angels, but have not **love**, I have become sounding brass or a tinkling symbol."

The second attribute of the Fruit of the Spirit is **joy**, χαρά (chara), and it has the same root as χάρις (charis), which means "grace." The third attribute is εἰρήνη (eirana), meaning "**peace**." So, together with ἀγάπη (agapa), these first three attributes of the Fruit of the Spirit are God's gift to us, and they give us serenity of mind and prepare us for service. With these attributes in mind, we might agree that the names "Grace" and "Irene," which come from the Greek, might be good names for girls.

The contrast between the Fruit of the Spirit and the works of the flesh is very important. They both start with love; however, the works of the flesh is a pseudo-love. Eros is the kind of love that Gomer had for Hosea (Hosea 3:1). In contrast, ἀγάπη is the kind of love that God had in sending His son to die for our sins (John 3:16).

Boy meets girl, and they "fall in love." They think that is all that is necessary—even though it might be a married spouse. So, they follow the desires of the flesh and start living together. After this relationship sours and they "fall out of love," they start looking for someone else. That is a pseudo-love affair. The genuine αγάπα love affair is a genuine love affair and it is a lifetime of commitment.

The first 3 attributes of the list of the works of the flesh are πορνεία (porneia), meaning "fornication," ἀκαθαρσία (akatharsia), meaning "impurity of motive, lewdness, unclean spirit," and ἀσέλγια (aselgia), meaning "sensuality, debauchery." These defile those who participate in such things. On the other hand, the spiritual man is blessed by love, joy, and peace. Whereas the Fruit of the Spirit leads to an abiding presence, the works of the flesh lead to the search for a "high," which results in depression. One leads to life, and the other leads to death.

The next three attributes of the Fruit of the Spirit are *patience, kindness, and goodness*. These give us an opportunity to enjoy life and to be a blessing to others. By contrast, some of the other attributes of the works of the flesh are "idolatry, abuse of drugs, hostility, strife, jealousy, fits of rage, self-seeking ambition, dissension, factions, and envy." These works of the flesh cause us to become bitter and to be a curse to others. One is a lifestyle that blesses, and the other is a lifestyle that curses. It becomes a part of us like our bloodstream, which constantly flows through our bodies.

The last three attributes of the Fruit of the Spirit are *faithfulness, meekness, and self-control*. These give character to the ones possessing them. In them, the mind is in control of the body, and life is meaningful. We are called to be faithful, not necessarily successful. Meekness means that we are living under the control of a higher power, and that means that our actions are blessings to us and to those around us.

On the other hand, the last attributes of the works of the flesh are drunkenness, carousing, and wild parties. These cause individuals to commit awful crimes, such as murder, robberies, adulteries, abuse of drugs, and many other crimes that cause destruction to the perpetrator and to those who are abused.

You may have heard the song entitled, "Don't worry—be happy." Most people would like to be happy, but, perhaps, most people are not happy. We may have been convinced that we can attain happiness if we achieve certain goals. We may think that if we had a better job, or better health, or marriage, or a million dollars, we would be happy. C.S. Lewis said, "We have No Right to Happiness. A right to happiness doesn't make much more sense than a right to be six feet tall, or to have a millionaire for a father, or to get good weather whenever you want to have a picnic."

There is something more important than happiness. It is joy. Happiness is the world's substitute for a spiritual reality which transcends happiness. Happiness is dependent on circumstances, but joy transcends them. Happiness involves one's environment—such as work, wealth, friends, social standing, or health—but joy is internal. Happiness is temporary; joy is an abiding presence. Happiness has to do with earthly things; joy has to do with spiritual things. Happiness is concerned about the here and now; joy is concerned about time and eternity. The Bible says very little about happiness, but it says much about joy. The works of the flesh may bring a little thrill to a dull life, but joy is the outgrowth or fruit of the indwelling presence of the Holy Spirit.

Remember that the works of the flesh can never bring an abiding joy; the happiness it may bring is only for a fleeting time. It is only the presence of the Holy Spirit that can bring this abiding joy. The master can and wants to give you the Holy Spirit, and it is through this Spirit that one can have the Fruit of the Spirit. If you do not have it, you can have it now, because this is the day of salvation if you turn to Him in faith.

The Good Samaritan
(Luke 10:25-37)

The Bible has many stories of different people. On one hand, it tells about wicked and violent people, such as Ahab and Jezebel; and, on the other hand, it tells about good people with superb character, such as Ruth from Moab and Esther during the Babylonian Captivity.

One of the greatest stories of all time is about the Samaritan who stopped to help the man who was dying somewhere on that rugged road between Jerusalem and Jericho. We have called it the story of The Good Samaritan, and certainly that is a beautiful title for describing that man of sterling character. We recognize him as good, even though the Bible just says, "a certain Samaritan." You may recall that the Jews detested the Samaritans. Most of the Jews, when traveling from Jerusalem to Galilee, would go around Samaria to get to their destination, rather than taking the shorter route that went through it.

The Jews and the Samaritans both came from the same heritage. They were the children of Jacob, or Israel. During the time of Solomon, the tribes of Israel were together, but during his reign, Solomon used his great wealth to live in excessive luxury, while his people were reduced to slavery. After his death, 10 of the 12 tribes of Israel seceded from the kingdom that Solomon had built. Solomon's son, Rehoboam, who ruled 922-915 B.C., foolishly refused to lighten the crushing burden of taxes and forced labor that Solomon had put on his people. When the people appealed to him to lighten their load, he followed his younger advisors, and his answer to them was,

"My father made your yoke heavy; I will make it even heavier. My father scourged

you with whips; I will scourge you with scorpions" (1 Kings 12:14).

As a result, Jeroboam, representing the Northern 10 tribes, caused a split in the kingdom, becoming the king over the Northern tribes, while Rehoboam remained king only over the tribes of Judah and Benjamin.

Jeroboam was ruler over Israel from 922 B.C. until 901 B.C., and the Northern Kingdom lasted 200 years after they seceded from the Davidic dynasty. The Assyrian ruler, Sargon II, later laid siege to Samaria and conquered it in 722 B.C. As was the Assyrian practice, the defeated people of Israel's Northern Kingdom were exiled to a variety of other countries, so Israel's "cream of the crop" was deported from their land. The Assyrians left only the poor and politically unimportant in the land and brought in many foreigners from other countries, which caused a mixture of the races. Israel lost most of her identity.

The Babylonians destroyed Jerusalem in 587 B.C., which was 135 years after Israel had fallen. The Babylonians did not have the same procedure for dealing with conquered nations as the Assyrians, but they did deport the people to a special place in Babylon. They were all together, so they could keep their identity, which had not been the case for Israel. Those in Babylonian captivity took the name of Jews from Judah, the strong tribe. Then, 70 years later under Cyrus, the Jews were permitted to return to their land and to rebuild Jerusalem and the Temple—the place for the worship of Jehovah.

The Samaritans worshipped at Mt. Gerizim, but the Jews worshipped at Mt. Zion. The Samaritans had only the Pentateuch, the first five books of the Old Testament, as their guide, but the Jews had the complete books of the Old

Testament. The two nations had drifted apart, and they did not like one another. In fact, they despised one another.

When the Jews came back to their land after the Babylonian Captivity, they did not want anything to do with the Samaritans. They even felt that to say the name, Samaritan, was enough to contaminate themselves. So, there was such a hatred between them that they had very little communication with one another.

Luke was the only Gentile writer of the New Testament. Without him, we would have never heard about the shepherds who told the message of the birth of Jesus and how they found him in the manger; we would not have heard the story of the Prodigal Son; and, we would not have the story of The Good Samaritan. Praise God for Dr. Luke!

The Bible does not actually call the Samaritan "Good." It only says that "a certain Samaritan traveler came by." However, it is easy for us to see why we call him "The Good Samaritan." For indeed, he displayed the qualities of goodness!

The story in the book of Luke about the The Good Samaritan begins with a theological question. We are told that a lawyer stood up and questioned Jesus. Evidently, his purpose was to embarrass Jesus and to put him down. The lawyer's question was, "Teacher, what must I do to inherit eternal life?"

Jesus responded to him with a simple, but profound, answer. He first asked him about the written Scriptures and what he thought about them. Jesus said, "What is written in the law? How do you understand it?"

The lawyer answered, "You shall love the Lord your God with all your heart, and with all your soul, and with all your strength, and with all your mind, and your neighbor as yourself?"

Jesus then told him that he had answered correctly and that if he did those things, he would live.

But, the lawyer, wishing to justify himself, said, "And who is my neighbor?"

Many people try to define a neighbor as someone special, leaving out most of mankind. They might think that it is the person who lives nearby, or maybe a person of their own race, or color, or social status.

The Greek word, πλησίον (plesion), is the neuter of πλησίος, α, ον, meaning "close," or "near." As an adverb, its meaning is, "(a) near, close-by; substantially, the neighbor, the one nearby, fellow man." So, the literal meaning is "the one who lives nearby." When I was a boy, I remember hearing people saying that our neighbor may not be the person who in nearby. I understood that the implication was that the person nearby may not be a person who would help me.

The lawyer's encounter with Jesus began with the question, "What must I do to inherit eternal life?" But, now the lofty heavenly theological question became a very practical earthly question, "And who is my neighbor?" Perhaps, the lawyer was expecting a simple answer, but Jesus did not answer with a direct response to the question. Instead, he told a story about a certain man going from Jerusalem to Jericho.

This man, going along the crooked road to Jericho, fell in with some robbers. The narrative seems to suggest that they were traveling together for awhile. But, somewhere along the way, the robbers overpowered the man and violently abused him. They left him half-dead; that is, he was dying! Soon, he would be dead if no one came by to help him.

First, by chance, a priest came down that way. It is literally true that he went "down," because Jerusalem is 2,500 feet above sea level, and Jericho is about 800 feet below sea level. That road is also rugged, being rocky, crooked, and narrow as it snakes its way from Jerusalem to Jericho. It could easily provide robbers with many hiding places.

As we begin our day, we make plans for what we shall do during the day. Perhaps, we think about how we can do a good job in the work that we are doing. We may visualize how we will arise in the morning, how we will discharge our responsibilities during the day, and how we will finish the day. But, we probably have not prepared to give money or time to the "freeloader," the sick, the hungry, or to anyone else, as we do our daily chores. But, during our daily activities, something may come up that will be more important than what we have planned for.

In the story before us, it was by chance that travelers passed by the dying man. It was coincidence how it happened, not being planned. It just happened.

The robbers had left, and there was the man dying beside the dusty road. The priest, who by chance was traveling down the same road, saw the dying man, but he passed on by, thinking that he did not have time to help him. His time was important. He may have been planning on performing a ritual or engaging in some other religious activity. If he touched a dead person, he would be disqualified to serve in the holy place. Regardless of his plans, it was not in his schedule of activities to deviate from his routine to help a dying man.

Secondly, a Levite came by that way and saw the man as he went by. He also had more important things to do than to waste his time with a stranger who was dying. He did not know the man, so why should he change his plans for the day to help him?

Before the man died, a Samaritan came passing by and saw him. This may have been the man's last chance to get help, but what would a despised Samaritan do for him? No Jew expected much from a Samaritan. Of the three travelers who had come upon the dying man, there was something about the Samaritan that caused him to go on the other side of the road and give aid. He had compassion in his heart.

The Samaritan was filled with compassion. The Greek word for compassion is σπλάγχνον (splagcnon). In referring to the body, it is defined as the "inward part," such as the heart, bowels, or liver. Literally, the word means, "intestines, viscera, inward parts" of the body, located in the belly (Acts 1:18). Figuratively, it refers to the deep, inner seat of tender emotions in the whole personality, such as the deep heartfelt emotion itself, with the context of "affection, love, deep feeling, compassion." Another way of translating it would be so say, "a gut feeling." This was the reason that the Samaritan went to give aid to the dying man.

Going to the dying man, the Samaritan bound up his wounds, pouring on oil and wine, and then he put him on his own beast and took him to Jericho. In addition to caring for the sick man, he left money with an innkeeper for additional aid in helping him. He told the innkeeper to care for him while he was gone, and if that was not enough money, he would pay him on his return trip.

After telling the story, Jesus asked the lawyer, "Which of these three do you think became neighbor to the one falling among the robbers?"

The lawyer would not even "dirty his mouth" by saying the word, "Samaritan," saying, "the one showing mercy to him."

Jesus said to him, "Go and you do likewise."

Notice that the question has been answered, but it is turned around. The question began with, "And who is my neighbor?" But Jesus turns it around and says, "Which of these three do you think became neighbor to the one falling among the robbers?"

So, the main question is not, "Who is my neighbor," but it is, "Who can I be a neighbor to?"

Have you ever seen a Good Samaritan? In the course of a lifetime, God gives us many opportunities to be a Good Samaritan to those who are needing help. And, no doubt, we have been helped by one. If we all had time, we could tell about how we have been rescued and how we have been able to help others.

One of my darkest days was when I left my wife and family early one morning to go to Misawa Air Base, Japan. I drove from Harlingen, Texas to San Francisco, California. From there, I flew to Tokyo, Japan and then traveled to Misawa, Japan. At the time, I was a Chaplain in the USAF. I knew no one there, and I did not know how the Japanese people would respond to me. The time was then 1959, and I had in mind the few years before when we had been in a bloody war with them. But my orders said, "Go." So, I went.

As military personnel, we traveled mainly by air to our destination in Japan, but our cars followed us by boat, taking several days to arrive behind us. Finally, the cars arrived at Hachinohe, Japan, which was several miles from where I was stationed at Misawa Air Base. Together with other military personnel, we went by bus over a crooked and dusty road that finally brought us over a hill of the city and down into the bay where our cars were waiting. After getting out of the bus and going to our cars, everyone was anxious to start their cars and return to our base. My car started, but it died. I tried several times, but it would not go. By that time, the bus had left, and the cars followed, leaving me behind. I can still see them going over the hill. In that direction the sun was just a little above the horizon.

Adjoining the city, there was a big field, and there were many Japanese people out and about, but I could not speak their language, and I wondered if they were friend or foe. After all, we had been enemies in war. Many weird thoughts came to me there as the sun was dropping over the western horizon. I was wondering whether the Japanese hated American people and how I was going to get back to the base. Actually, the roaming of the bus had turned me around, and I did not even know which direction was the way home! My family and my friends were almost half a world away from me. That was before cell phones, so I had no way of communication, and even if I should get my car started, I would not know how to get back to the base. I thought, "What can I do?" I could pray, so I did. It was a helpless feeling. The sun was nearing the horizon and I was alone in a foreign land. I think that it was one of the most desolate experiences of my lifetime.

Just before the sun dropped down below the horizon, I heard a noise and then saw a helicopter landing near my car. It was a helicopter pilot coming to get his car. He was glad to help me. He started his car and took me home! I do not remember his name, but I do remember that he was a kind, considerate officer. He was about my age, and he was black. It was an experience that I shall never forget. He was The Good Samaritan that rescued me in a foreign land. I shall ever be grateful to him.

Jesus ended his encounter with the lawyer by saying, "Go, and do likewise!" May that be a goal of our lives!

The Meekness of Wisdom
(James 3:1-18)

In the expression, "the Meekness of Wisdom," as found in the book of James, there are two very important Greek words, πραΰτης (prautes), and σοφία (sophia). Let us examine the meaning of the words, starting with σοφία which means "wisdom." In general, this means the ability to use knowledge for correct behavior. But also by human wisdom, we often mean cleverness, as opposed to the supreme intelligence of God and Christ, who is the embodiment of God. Sometimes, the word is used of earthly wisdom, which is devilish, and other times it is used as the heavenly wisdom that comes from above. Today, we are talking about the pure wisdom that comes from above.

The other word, πραΰτης, generally meaning "meekness," is hard to translate into English. The noun form is used 3 times in the Greek N.T. Quoting from James 1:21, "Therefore put away all filthiness and every vicious excess and in **meekness** receive the implanted word, which is able to save your souls." In 1 Peter 3:15-16, it says, "…always be ready to make a defense to everyone who asks you concerning the hope that is in you, but with **meekness** and reverence, and with a good conscience, so that those who slander you may be put to shame because of your good behavior in Christ." Then, in the text before us in James 3:13, it says, "Who is wise and understanding among you? By his good lifestyle let him show his good works in the **meekness** of wisdom."

There are also 3 adjectives that express this thought. Matthew 5:5 says, "Blessed are the **meek**, for they shall inherit the earth." 1 Peter 3:3-4 says, "Let not your beauty come from the outward adornment, such as braided hair, the wearing of gold jewelry and fine clothing, but by the hidden person of the heart, an incorruptible *meek* and quiet spirit, which is of great value before God." In Matthew 21:5, it says, "…Behold, the king is coming to you, *meek* and riding on a donkey…." So Jesus rode into Jerusalem riding a donkey. His first order of business was to clean the temple. Jesus entered the temple and drove out all who sold and bought in the temple.

I have not found another word in English that is synonymous with the word "meek." So, what does meek mean? It is not humility; neither is it arrogance. It is not necessarily gentle, but it does express itself in a patient submission to offense and is always free from malice and desire for revenge. It is assumed by many that when a man is meek, it is because he cannot help himself. In Numbers, we read that Moses was by far the meekest man on the face of the earth. Jesus was not weak, but we are told that he had the infinite resources of God at his command. Negatively expressed, meekness is the opposite of self-assertion and self-interest. The meek person is not concerned about self; he is concerned about doing the dictates of that higher power. The military has a good word that expresses the meaning of the word—it is discipline. The general gives the order, and the private soldier in the foxhole carries out his command.

Wisdom gives the command, and meekness carries out the orders. The day when Jesus rode the donkey into Jerusalem, he went to the temple to carry out the Father's will. He was meek, because he was obedient to the Father's will. When Jesus entered the temple, he drove out all who sold and bought in the temple, and he overturned the tables of the moneychangers and the seats of those who sold pigeons. It was not a quiet and humble spirit that caused

Jesus to drive out of the temple those who were making it a house of merchandise. And, he probably insulted them when he told them that they were making the house of prayer into a den of robbers. The significant question for Jesus and for me and for you is, "What does God want us to do today, now?"

In connection with wisdom, James has much to say about the tongue. The chapter begins by telling us that only a few should be teachers, because the teacher will be judged with greater strictness. The tongue can be a blessing or a curse. It can be an instrument for good or for evil. If we do not stumble in the use of our tongues, we are mature (the word is sometimes translated "perfect"). James says that if we are able to control our tongues, we are able to control our whole body.

Then, James gives us two illustrations that tell us how delicate the tongue is, comparing it to the bits in the horse's mouth and the small rudder of a ship. I grew up on a farm, so I am very familiar with the horse and the bridle. The bridle fits around the head of the horse, and the bits are in the mouth of the horse. There are slender leather lines about an inch thick, called reins, that extend from the bridle of the horse to the driver of the buggy, which help to control the horse's movements.

I am reminded of a buggy ride that I had as a boy, which I shall never forget. My mother, my grandmother, and I planned on that occasion to go for a visit with our relatives, Uncle Jake Parrish and his wife, Aunt Amy, and their two children, Herbert and Hazel Parrish. The distance to their farm was about four and a half miles on the road from our home. Our mode of transportation was a one-seated buggy, with a canvas top over our heads. I think that it was "Old Ider," our mule, that was pulling the buggy.

Leaving early in the morning, we planned to return in the afternoon or early evening, because there were no lights on the buggy. Old Ider was healthy and ready to go, so we had plenty of "horse power" to make the trip.

It was a beautiful morning, as my grandma Wilton took the reins and became the "chauffeur" for our buggy ride. Not far from our farm houses, our route took us past Easter Hill, which was about a half mile away. At the top of the hill, there was a very sharp drop into a valley on one side of the narrow road that passed over the hill, and as we went over the hill, something unexpected happened. Old Ider got her tail over the reins, which was what grandma used to control the steering for the buggy. That was like losing the steering rod in a car, and the result was that the driver lost control of the vehicle. As a consequence, Old Ider began running away with the buggy, going over the hill at lightening speed. At the foot of the hill, where there was a curve in the road, the buggy ended upside down in a large bar ditch.

At first, it had seemed to me like an exciting buggy ride, but the next thing I remember was that we were in the bar ditch, with the buggy turned upside down on top of us. Old Ider left the buggy behind and finished her run, ending up in Sam Easter's cotton patch. We climbed out of the bar ditch and walked up the steep hill and returned home. No one was hurt, but I was disappointed that I did not get to play with my cousin Herbert that day. It all happened because the bits in the horse's mouth were not under the control of the driver.

Likewise, James tells us that our tongues can get out of our control, and as a result can cause much damage. The tongue, like a tiny speck of fire, can cause devastation. That speck of fire can cause a huge forest to go up in flames.

Many animals can be tamed, but no one can subdue the tongue; it is an unruly evil and full of deadly venom. We are not to use the tongue to praise God and then use the same tongue to curse man. A fountain does not gush forth with fresh water, and then with salt water, from the same source. Neither can the tongue do likewise.

A major component of the meekness of wisdom is love. When meekness is under control of love, we are led into a perfect relationship to others. One of the Greek words for love is φιλέω (phileo), which is used 25 times in the Greek N.T. It means "to love," whether referring to persons or things. In the KJV of the Bible, it is translated as "love," or "kiss." When the prefix, κατά (kata), is added to the word, the meaning is "to kiss fervently or affectionately," and when it is in the imperfect tense, it means to do so repeatedly. The word, καταφιλέω (kataphileo), is the word that is used by Judas in the garden of Gethsemane when he betrayed Jesus, and it is the word the Father used when the Prodigal Son came home. It is used 6 times in the Greek N.T., but it is used only on 4 occasions.

One of those occasions was in Acts 20:37, when Paul was on his way to Jerusalem with the offering for the poor, but he stopped by Ephesus on his way to Jerusalem. The elders of the church met him there, and when he prepared to leave them, the elders "fell on Paul's neck and **kissed** him."

Another instance was in Luke 7:38,45, when Jesus accepted an invitation to dine in a Pharisee's home. A sinful woman of the city heard that Jesus was there and was reclining at a table. She brought an alabaster box of ointment, and standing behind Jesus at his feet, she began weeping, and she wet his feet with her tears, wiping them with the hair of her head, **kissing** his feet, and anointing them with the ointment.

Let us look further at the occasions of Judas kissing Jesus and the Father kissing the Prodigal. The word, καταφιλέω, normally was the expression of deep emotional love. The kiss of Judas was a kiss of deception. When Judas betrayed Jesus, he led the mob with swords and clubs from the chief priests, scribes, and elders, in the darkness of the night to the Garden of Gethsemane. He said, "The one I kiss is he; seize him and take him away under guard. Then, he immediately came to Jesus and said, 'Rabbi!' And he **fervently kissed** him" (Matthew 26:48-49; Mark 14:44-45).

When the Prodigal came home, it was a beautiful reception. He had demanded his inheritance when he left home. After a time with the wrong kind of people, living in sin with the prostitutes and other dregs of society, his money ran out. He ended up feeding swine. He wanted to eat the pods he was feeding to the swine, but no one gave him anything. He was not at the altar of a luxurious church when he repented and decided to return home, no longer as a son, but as a hired hand. Rather, it was while he was in the pigpen. On his return home, while he was still at a far distance, his father saw him, and moved by compassion, he ran to him and fell upon his neck and **fervently kissed** him.

The kiss of Judas was a fake and a deception, used as a sign for the betrayal of his best friend. On the other hand, the kiss of the Prodigal by the Father was a pure kiss of compassionate love. We can learn from this that our words and our thoughts must be compatible with one another; otherwise, our words will be the expression of the hypocrite.

So, the same word, on one hand, can express the awful deception of hypocrisy, and, one the other hand, it can be the precious expression of a deep compassionate love. We need to watch our tongues, because the words we use are important; but, the true expression of sincerity is even more important.

There are two kinds of wisdom; one is earthly, natural, and devilish; and, the other is heavenly. The earthly wisdom is the kind that Solomon had in his latter years. His kingdom was so luxurious and mighty that it became a showcase for the world. Even the Queen of Sheba came a long way to see the display of Solomon in his wealth and luxury. She left saying, "The half has not been told!" And yet, Solomon made slaves of his people, and he had a thousand wives and concubines. His earthly wisdom led to the downfall of his kingdom. Surely, it was devilish and destructive.

The wisdom that comes from above is the wisdom that we need to seek after. When we have found it, then, by meekness, we bring it to pass. Proverbs 9:10 says, "The fear of the Lord is the beginning of wisdom, and knowledge of the Holy One is understanding." This wisdom that comes down from above is for all who seek it with all their hearts. It is not inherited from parent to child; no schools are able to impart it; money cannot by it; it is not earned by hard work; but, it is the most precious gift that anyone can receive.

If you have bitter jealousy and selfish ambition, do not boast about it, because it is earthly, natural and demon-like, and with it comes disorder and every worthless action. But the wisdom from above is pure, peaceable, gentle, reasonable, and full of mercy and good fruits. The harvest of righteousness is sown in peace by the peacemakers.

The Meekness of Wisdom causes us to grow in the grace and knowledge of our Lord and Savior Jesus Christ. God wants you to have it.

Things to remember about wisdom:

Fear of the Lord is the beginning of wisdom.
Wisdom is not purchased by money.
The schools cannot impart it.
Only the poor in spirit are eligible for it.
Commit your life to Jesus and receive it now.

The gift of wisdom is free, but it will be the most blessed gift that you have ever received. Blessings on you!

The Rich Farmer
(Luke 12:13-21)

Jesus had been talking about eternal things. He said, "...do not fear those who can kill the body but can do nothing more. But I warn you to fear the one who...has authority to cast into hell. Yes, I tell you, fear that one!" (Luke 12:4-5). He also said, "...all who confess me before men, the Son of Man will confess before the angels of God, but those denying me before men will be denied before the angels" (Luke 12:8-9).

While Jesus was talking about eternal life, there was a man in the crowd who spoke out to Jesus. He said, "Teacher, tell my brother to divide the inheritance with me" (Luke 12:13). Jesus told him that was not why he came. He came to seek and to save that which was lost.

Then Jesus said, "Watch for and guard against all covetousness, for the abundant life is not determined by one's possessions" (Luke 12:15). Then Jesus told them a parable.

There was a rich man whose land produced abundantly. He thought within himself, "What shall I do, because I have no place to store my grain?" (Luke 12:17).

Then he said to himself, "This I will do: I will tear down my old barns and build larger ones, and I will store all my grain and my goods there. And I will say to my soul, 'Soul, you have laid up many goods for many years, relax, eat, drink, and be merry'" (Luke 12:18-19).

But God said to him, "Foolish man! This night your life is demanded from you, and who will get your possessions?" (Luke 12:20).

So it is for those who lay up treasures for themselves but are not rich toward God. The rich farmer had been a very progressive farmer. He was a hard worker and an intelligent manager. There is no indication that he was a thief, or a womanizer, or that he had ever been a drunk, or addicted to drugs. The world would acclaim him as a success.

We can imagine that if there had been a Jerusalem Gazette, the rich farmer would have had much praise in the daily obituary section. Here was a prosperous man who became an example for the younger generation to follow. He was in good health, and he had recently retired. But, he died—perhaps, due to a heart attack.

We have rich men and rich women in every generation. Abraham was a wealthy man, but he was called a friend of God. Joseph became one of the wealthiest men in Egypt; yet, he was a very godly person. Job was the wealthiest man in the land of Uz. Job had 7,000 sheep, 3,000 camels, 500 yoke of oxen, 500 donkeys, and many servants. He was the greatest man among all the people of the East. And, the Bible says that "This man was blameless and upright; he feared God and shunned evil" (Job 1:1). When Satan accused Job, God defended him by saying, "There is no one on earth like him, he is blameless and upright, a man who fears God and shuns evil" (Job 1:8). Zacchaeus was a wealthy man when he climbed up into a tree to see Jesus as he passed by. When he met Jesus, his ideas about wealth changed. Then he was ready to use his wealth to glorify God. The fact that the rich farmer was wealthy did not condemn him. His problem was much deeper than that. His problem was that he had a lifestyle of self-centeredness.

Some wealthy men are good, and some are bad. So, what makes the difference? In the story of the Rich Farmer, Jesus said that he was a fool. Therefore, what was the problem of this Rich Farmer? I think that he made three mistakes. First of all, he was more interested in himself than he was of his neighbor. He only addressed his problem in reference to himself. He seems to have been obsessed with himself. He was saying to himself, "What shall I do? My barns are too small for all my grain. If I can build larger barns, I can hoard it all. So, that is what I will do. I will build my barns so big that I can save all my grain."

There must have been poor people who were starving for lack of food. But, he was only concerned about himself. He was the center of his little world. He had no interest in helping the needy. His motto must have been, "Bigger barns, more security. What else does a person need? Who needs friends when a person has the wealth to buy the community?"

The Rich Farmer's second mistake was that he considered the physical more important than the spiritual. His donkey's need was satisfied by having enough grain, but just as in the temptation of Jesus with Satan (Matthew 4:4), Jesus said, "Man shall not live by bread alone, but by every word that comes from the mouth of God." There is always a need for bread, but bread is not man's greatest need. Man's greatest needs are in the realm of spiritual things. Physical wealth can never be a source of eternal joy.

The Rich Farmer thought that he had it made. With his barns full he said to his soul, "Soul, you have laid up many goods for many years, relax, eat, drink, and be merry." He must have considered all the hard work it had taken to amass his wealth, and now it was time to sit back in a rocking chair and eat and drink and do the things that thrills the flesh and brings excitement in merrymaking.

We read in the daily newspaper of a college student who killed his ex-girlfriend and her brother. After first being faced with a lifetime in prison or the death penalty, he was finally given a death sentence. Those in prison have food to eat and shelter from the cold and the heat, but freedom has been taken away from them. Most of them long for freedom, again. Even so, their great need it not just freedom from prison, but freedom from sin and the haunting of a lifetime of regret and debauchery. Regardless of the situation, God's grace is adequate for a lifestyle of victory and blessedness. Paul wrote some of his best epistles while he was in prison!

Many people today are living lives only of the flesh. They think that if they can keep the flesh satisfied, that is what life is all about. We are told what the works of the flesh are in Galatians 5:19-21, which leads to devastation. On the other hand, we learn what the fruit of the Spirit is in Galatians 5:23. One leads to death; but, the other leads to life. It is a tragic mistake to be more concerned about the physical than about the spiritual.

The third mistake that the Rich Farmer made was that he was more concerned about his time on earth than about eternity. He seemed to think that life had just begun for him, and that now he could really begin to live. Some people live as if this life is all there is. Some make plans for education, with most hoping for a good college education. Then, most people plan for marriage and for rearing a family. Then, they think about saving up for retirement. Is that as far as most people plan for? Is that far enough?

The Rich Farmer thought that he had grain for many years, and he assumed that he had many years to party. It was that very night that God spoke to him, possibly during the time of his merrymaking. What a tragic message God had for this successful businessman. God said, "Foolish man! This night your life is demanded from you, and who will get your possessions?"

What a tragedy! This man had worked hard to store up earthly treasures to enjoy! He had given his lifework to the accumulation of material wealth! He had not been interested in eternal security, only security for Time. His plans were only for this short time of life.

Then, Jesus summed up the parable by saying, "So it is to those who lay up treasures for themselves but are not rich toward God" (Luke 12:21). So, Jesus has a message for us today. Are we rich toward God? If not, we are in the same position as the Rich farmer.

So, that leads to a very personal question. Where are our riches? Do we have earthly riches, which are not very important?   Do we have heavenly riches, which are important? What is our thrust of motivation in life? Is it to lay up earthly treasures, or is it to lay up heavenly treasures?

Then, the question is "how do we become rich toward God?" I think that we can turn the equation around and say that we must be concerned about others rather than to be self-centered, that we must be concerned more about the spiritual than the physical, and that we must be more concerned about eternity than about time.

We all have goals in life. It is necessary for us to make provisions for the flesh. We need food and drink to maintain a functioning body. And, the body of the flesh is not evil. Our bodies can be instruments of sin, or they can be the temple of the Holy Spirit. Paul writes to the Romans (Romans 6:11-13), "So also consider yourselves to be dead to sin, but alive to God in Christ Jesus. Therefore do not let sin reign in your mortal bodies, so that you obey the desires of your natural self, and do not continue to offer the members of your body to sin as weapons of unrighteousness, but offer yourselves to God as those alive from the dead, and your members as weapons of righteousness to God."

So, work is good, and it is wise to go to school and develop skills and plan for the future; but, as we work and plan for laying up treasures on earth, we should be more concerned about laying up treasures in heaven. The Rich Farmer was only concerned about filling his barns and making bigger ones. There must have been some hungry people that he could have helped. God called him a fool, because he spent his time working only for himself, and when "his little day" was completed, he had laid up no heavenly treasures. What a pathetic situation!

Where are we today? Where are our treasures? We might go to the courthouse to check on our deeds and earthly treasures, or we might go to the bank and check on our checking account. What is your heavenly account? And, do you have money in your spiritual bank? Have we made some good deposits there, lately?

Let's see if we can find some examples of people in the Bible. Jesus told an interesting story about a certain man traveling from Jerusalem to Jericho, who was attacked by robbers and was left stripped, beaten, and left for dead.

While he was lying on the side of the road, a priest and a Levite came by, but then when they saw him, they passed him by. Then, a certain Samaritan came by, but when he saw the dying man, he had compassion on him and ministered to him. After bandaging his wounds, he took him to an inn and paid the innkeeper for his accommodations. Before the Samaritan left to continue on his journey, he told the innkeeper to take care of the wounded man, and he told him he would pay his bill when he returned. Evidently, he was a businessman with a mission to fulfill, but he had time to help the dying man. Each of the three men had a job to do, and each one had a chance that day to lay up treasures in heaven, but only one took advantage of that opportunity. I think that the good Samaritan made a good deposit in the heavenly bank that day.

David was King of Israel, and he had been blessed of God in many ways, but one day he committed adultery with Bathsheba, the wife of Uriah the Hittite, one of his most faithful commanders. To cover up his sin, David had Uriah killed. The Lord sent Nathan, the prophet, to confront David, the king. Nathan told David about two men in a certain town, one rich and the other poor. The rich man had many sheep and cattle. The poor man had only one little ewe lamb, which had grown up with him and his children. The lamb shared his food, drank from his cup, and even slept in his arms. It was like one of the family. When a traveler came visiting, the rich man did not take one of his many sheep to prepare a meal for the traveler, but he took the ewe lamb that belonged to the poor man and prepared it for the traveler.

When David heard the story, he burned with anger against the rich man, and he said to Nathan, "As surely as the Lord lives, the man who did this deserves to die! He must pay for that lamb four times over, because he did such a thing and had no pity."

Nathan said to David, "You are the man!" It took courage to tell this to the king, who had the power of life or death, that he was judged for his wicked deeds and that the sword would never depart from his house, because he despised the Lord and took the wife of Uriah the Hittite for his own. I think Nathan made a good deposit and laid up treasures in heaven that day.

King Nebuchadnezzar made an image of gold, which was ninety feet high and nine feet wide, and he set it up in Dura, a province of Babylon. He demanded that everyone, at the sound of the musical instruments, must fall down and worship the image. Those who refused would be thrown into a blazing furnace.

Shadrach, Meshach, and Abednego, who were Jewish refugees in the king's service, refused to fall down and worship the image. They were brought before Nebuchadnezzar, and they replied to him, "O Nebuchadnezzar, we do not need to defend ourselves before you in this matter. If we are thrown into the blazing furnace, the God we serve is able to save us from it, and he will rescue us from your hand, O king. But even if he does not, we want you to know, O king, that we will not serve your gods or worship the image of gold you have set up" (Daniel 3:16-18).

Then, Nebuchadnezzar was furious with Shadrach, Meshach, and Abednego, and he ordered the furnace heated seven times hotter than usual. He ordered his soldiers to throw Shadrach, Meshach, and Abednego into the furnace. The king was surprised to see 4 men in the furnace, and he said, "...the fourth looks like a son of the gods" (Daniel 3:25).

When King Nebuchadnezzar saw that the fire had not harmed their bodies, nor singed the hair of their heads, nor scorched their robes, he praised the God of Shadrach, Meshach, and Abednego and gave them back their jobs and promoted them. However, their greater promotion was that they were laying up treasures in heaven.

So, how do we lay up treasures in heaven? It is not by the works of the flesh, because the flesh is only interested in the temporary. To become rich toward God, it must be through the Spirit. Paul tells us in his letter to the Romans (12:1-2) what it is to lay up treasures in heaven, saying, "I appeal to you therefore, brothers, by the mercies of God, to present your bodies as a living sacrifice, holy and well-pleasing which is your reasonable service, and do not be conformed to this age, but be transformed by the renewing of the mind, so that you may be able to discern the will of God, which is good, well-pleasing, and perfect."

If we are conformed to this world, we will never know what the finer things of life are all about. When we lay our bodies on the altar, we will be ready to use our bodies as instruments of righteousness. We are to be transformed by the renewing of the mind in prayer. The Greek word for being transformed is μεταμορφόομαι (metamorphaomai). We think of the worm that is transformed into a beautiful butterfly. It is the people who are transformed who can discern the will of God, which is good, well-pleasing, and perfect.

To lay up treasures in heaven, we must have a healthy concern for others. Our hard hearts must to be softened. There is no place for hatred, hostility, Jealousy, envy, and cynicism; but, now there must be love, compassion, good will, and a desire to become involved in the lives of others.

If we fast-forward to Judgment Day, we can see the importance of being concerned about the welfare of others. We read about that day in Matthew 25:34-46, which recounts that, "Then the king will say to those on the right, 'Come, you blessed of my Father, inherit the kingdom which has been prepared from the foundation of the world. For I was hungry and you fed me, I was thirsty and you gave me something to drink, I was a stranger and you entertained me, I was naked and you clothed me, I was sick and you visited me, I was in prison and you came to me.' " On the other hand, the ones who did not show proper concern for those who were in need were cast into eternal fire. We lay up treasures in heaven when we minister to others.

Where do you stand today? Is your heavenly bank account in good shape? Are you more interested in earthly treasures than heavenly treasures? Dr. George W. Truitt was one of the greatest of pastors and preachers. He was pastor of the First Baptist Church of Dallas for 47 years. He often went out to a ranch in West Texas for a revival meeting with the cowboys. On one occasion, he was the guest of one of the wealthy ranchers. There was an upstairs balcony that wrapped around the entire house. When he was showing Dr. Truitt his ranch, the rancher took him to the north side of the balcony and, raising his hand toward the north direction, he said, "My land extends as far as you can see to the north." Then, he went likewise to the west, south, and east sides of the balcony, and at each stop he extended his hand to that direction and said, "My land extends as far as you can see." Then, Dr. Truitt raised his hand and extended it toward heaven and asked him about his treasures in that direction of spiritual things.

Remember, God called the Rich Farmer a fool. He was self-centered, with no concern about others. If we are going to be rich toward God, we must be concerned about others. The Rich Farmer was concerned about the material things, but not about spiritual matters. If we are going to be rich toward God, we must be concerned about spiritual things, because God is spirit, and those who worship him must worship him in spirit and truth (John 4:24). The Rich Farmer was concerned about time rather than eternity. If we are going to be rich toward God, we must be concerned about eternity. Just to plan for work and retirement is not enough. We must plan for eternity.

Today is the day of salvation. Prepare for eternity by trusting in the Lord today. The message of the gospel is for now. Receive Him in your heart now, and then at the end of life the Master will say, "Well done, good and faithful servant, enter into the joy of the Lord!"

The Sacredness of Living
(John 9:1-7)

As Joshua was preparing his people to enter the Promised Land, he emphasized that "ye have not passed this way before" (Joshua 3:4). There is an old Quaker motto that says: "I shall pass through this world but once. Any good, therefore, that I can show to any human being, let me do it now, let me not defer nor neglect it, for I shall not pass this way again."

What an awesome responsibly it is to live every day, every minute, with the opportunity of using every minute honoring God and being a blessing to others! Time is a precious gift from the Almighty who created us. Let us never kill it, waste it, or abuse it; but, may our commitment be to the Almighty who gives us the wisdom to know how to use it wisely!

One day when Jesus was passing along the way, he saw a man blind from birth. His disciples asked him, saying, "Rabbi, who sinned, this man or his parents, that he was born blind?" Jesus answered, "Neither this man nor his parents sinned; but that the works of God might be manifest in him, it is necessary for us to work the works of the one having sent me while it is day; the night comes when no one can work" (John 9:2-4).

When the disciples saw the man who had been born blind, they wanted to talk about the reason for his pitiful condition. Many times we fall into the trap of just talking about the problems of others. It might go something like this: He is no good because he came from a bad family; he is cursed because of his evil life; he has a history of alcohol and drugs and he will never be good for anything! Such evaluations are never edifying.

When Jesus saw the man born blind, he was not concerned about the cause of blindness; he was interested in helping the person who was in need. The disciples were only interested in philosophizing on the cause of the man's blindness. Jesus said that this is an opportunity for us to work with God and minister to the man in need. In this incident, Jesus gave us guidelines in carrying out His ministry.

To live is to exert influence. The "real" person we are is more important than what we do. Some people have more influence that others, but we all have an influence that is flowing out constantly. It may be around the dining table with children and their parents, talking about their neighbor; it may be in the family car with the kids on the way to church when the driver goes through a stoplight; it may be in the classroom with the teacher instructing a class of students. The unconscious influences in each example may be more profound than the conscious influence. In stormy weather, the rain, wind, and thunder may be frightening, but the constant pull of gravity has the power to give us stability.

So, whether it is in the home, in the church, in the school, in the political office, or in the community, everyone is exerting both conscious and unconscious influences. I am convinced that the unconscious influence is more important. If the influence is bad, the home may be destroyed, the church may be split, the school may be crippled, and the politics may be soured. On the other hand, if it is a good influence, the home will be strengthened, the church will be glorified, the school will be honored, and in politics, the people will be blessed. Some people impart a bad influence while others have a good influence, but everyone has an influence flowing from him/her all through life.

Even the babies in the cradle are influenced by their parents or others who attend to their needs. This is a time when prejudices and other attributes are learned and become a part of their lives. Children at a very young age learn values in life, whether they may be good or bad, so much so that they can be either cursed or blessed by them. Attitudes, complexes, ideas, and ideals are caught by them, more by unconscious influence than by direct teaching.

Since we all have an influence that is constantly blessing or cursing the people we daily associate with, living should be treated as a sacred trust. Since life is so sacred and we are creatures of habit, we should realize that our thought patterns, whether good or bad, influence how our lifestyle manifests itself. If we are filled with jealousy, hostility, or other attributes of our old nature, we need to change. If our influence is going to be good, we must reflect the goodness of God in our lives. The light of love and compassion should flow from our lives rather the negative attributes of desires of the flesh. What an awesome challenge and responsibility we have!

How do we develop a way of maintaining good thoughts? Some suggestions are to read good books that encourage godly thinking, to watch TV programs or movies that are morally and creatively uplifting, and to talk about things that are worthy of our time rather than engaging in gossip and faultfinding. When we use our energies "to redeem the time" that God has given us, we are developing a lifestyle of acceptable thinking.

To put it another way, we need to think positively rather than negatively. If we spend our time thinking about failing, we will usually fail, but if we spend our time thinking about our abilities and our blessings, we will be much better prepared in our pursuit of a life of usefulness.

If we practice thinking negative thoughts, we will get in a rut that will be difficult to dig out of. What we do and think about today will spill over into tomorrow. The rut of worries, anxieties, depression, hostilities, and satisfaction of the flesh can be hard to overcome, but with the grace of God it can be done.

Dr. Donald Barker, who taught psychology for 35 years at Texas A&M University, said, "You cannot have a good day with a bad attitude, and you cannot have a bad day with a good attitude." So, by extension, how can we have a good life? It is not by wealth, nor by power, nor by status, nor by education, nor by health, but it is by the attitude of the mind. "Whatsoever a man thinks in his heart, so is he." We do not need to have an idle mind, but we do need to have a mind of godly thoughts. It is through God's grace that we can receive the power of lofty thoughts. We can live by faith instead of worry and anxieties; we can thank God for the blessings of life and rejoice in them rather than be distressed by a grumpy attitude; we can love and appreciate our friends rather than live in hostility toward our enemies.

If we do not have the godly attitude, we can ask God to give it to us. He wants to give it to us, but we must be willing to surrender to his rule for our lives. As the Scriptures tells us in James 4:7-8, "Submit yourselves therefore to God. Resist the devil, and he will flee from you. Draw near to God, and He will draw near to you." To have fellowship with God gives us a good attitude to live by.

One of the reasons that life is so sacred is that it gives us precious memories. Some people do not have good memories. That may be due to a wasted life, or a prison term with years of confinement, or it may be the result of destruction of family relations. So, what is the answer? The sinner needs to ask God's forgiveness. If he comes in the right attitude of surrendering to him, God will forgive him. There may be some things that the forgiven sinner should also do after he is forgiven. He/she may need to make restitution for damages that he/she has caused to others. But then there can come a time to create precious memories. If our problem is that we have practiced the habit of using the tongue for cursing and evil speaking, we need to change our lifestyle, because life is too sacred for us to abuse it with evil thoughts.

Each day of our lives is a precious blessing, because it offers another opportunity for building memories for the future. Whether our memories become precious or terrifying depends upon our actions today. Deeds of kindness and benevolence rise up to bless us. What we do today will spill over into tomorrow, and if we do good things today, we can start tomorrow with the pleasing lingering thoughts of the past day. Every act is an act of eternity; every thought is a thought of eternity; and, every deed is a deed of eternity.

Life is also sacred because Judgment Day is coming. The wages of sin is death, but the gift of God is eternal life. In that day we will remember what we did in this life. In God's "computer program," everything is eternally recorded on His hard drive. Every good deed and every good thought is rewarded, and every bad deed has its punishment. We can be forgiven of our sins, but consequences follow every evil deed, and blessings follow every good deed. Sin causes much evil in this life. Jesus tells us in Matthew 12:36, that "...on judgment day men will be held accountable for every idle word they speak...." The Bible tells us that punishment for some is in the present life, but for others it reserved for judgment day.

So, where are your treasures? If they exist only on this earth, God calls us a fool (Luke 12:20-21). If we have no heavenly treasures laid up, we need to be desperately giving our lives to spiritual things, because the earthly treasures are only temporary. All of us who are still in the land of the living can use the time we have to lay up treasures in heaven. When we have surrendered to Him, resisting the devil and causing him to flee, then God will show us how to lay up treasures in heaven. We cannot change the past, but we can prepare for the future by doing God's will in the ever present now. On that day, may the Good Lord bless you with the words, "Well done, good and faithful servant, enter into the joy of the Lord!"

The War
(James 4:1-17)

Wars seem to never cease. Wars are always going on somewhere in the world. We pray and hope for peace to come. But, if we have temporary peace in one part of the world, war breaks out in another part of the world. So, it looks like we will have wars and rumors of wars until the end of time.

James tells us about the personal war that is our lifestyle. Feuds and fights are a part of us, because a war is going on in our bodies all the time. In James 4:1-3, he asks about the source of our wars:

"(1) What is the source of your feuds and fights among you? Is it not because of the war of your lusts in your bodies? (2) You covet, but you do not have, so you commit murder; and you are jealous but you cannot acquire, so you fight and quarrel. You do not have, because you do not ask. (3) You ask, but you do not receive, because you ask with evil motives, to indulge in sensual pleasures."

There are two Greek words used to describe this personal battle. One is πόλεμος (polemos), and the other is μάχη (mache). They are translated in a variety of ways, such as: "feuds and fights, feuds and struggles, fighting and quarrels, conflict and wrangles, wars and fighting, fights and quarrels, conflicts and quarrels, fighting and quarrelling."

Πόλεμος literally means "armed conflict," or "war." Sometimes, it is used as a single engagement fought with weapons. Figuratively and negatively, it can mean "the battle within a community, or strife, quarrel, or conflict."

Μάχη literally means "physical combat," or "a contest fought with weapons in a battle, conflict, or fight"; in the N.T., figuratively and in the plural, it is used to describe battles fought with words only, such as disputes, quarrels, or strife. So, πόλεμος refers to "the chronic state or campaign of war," while μάχη refers to "the separate battles" we encounter.

Another word, στρατευομένων (strateuomenon), is used for soldiering or carrying on a campaign to fight in a military battle.

The battleground of our spiritual war is the abode of the passions. So, the battle goes on. There is the desire for things that cannot be lawfully obtained, so murder is committed. And, there are lusts for things that are unlawful and immoral that one cannot obtain. So, the war rages on. The passions of the flesh fight against the standards of fair play and morality. Paul tells us what the works of the flesh are: "fornication, uncleanness, sensuality, …dissensions, factions, envy, drunkenness, carousing, and the like" (Galatians 5:19-21).

James says that you do not have, because you do not ask, and if you do ask, it is for the wrong motives, with the purpose of indulging in the fleshly pleasures of the flesh. So, when they are withheld, it is for the good of the one asking for them.

In James 4:4-6, we are told what the problem is:

"(4) You adulteresses! Do you not know that the friendship of the world is hostility toward God? So whoever chooses to be a friend of the world becomes an enemy of God. (5) Or do you think that Scripture vainly says, 'The spirit which dwells in you has envious desires'; (6) but

***he gives greater grace. Thus the Scripture
says, 'God resists the arrogant, but gives
grace to the humble.' "***

The Greek word, μοιχαλίς (moichalis), means
"adulteress, one who is unfaithful in the marriage vows."
The term became a figure of speech in the O.T. to indicate
unfaithfulness to God and to the practice of idolatry, but
here the false god is the world. There are two other
important words in this paragraph. The first one is φιλία
(philia), which means "friendship." It involves the idea of
loving, as well as of being loved. The other word, ἔχθρα
(echthra), means "enmity or active hostility." Both words
are used in our relationship to the world. Friendship to the
world means hostility toward God.

Where is your friendship? Do you love God, or do
you love the world? What thrills you most, your favorite ball
team getting a touchdown, or your wayward friend finding
his/her way back to the Father's house? Is it going to the
bar and drinking intoxicating liquors, or is it going to the
sanctuary of the Lord and being filled with the Spirit of
Christ? Do you love the works of the flesh more than the
fruit of the Spirit? Do you have a selfish, envious spirit
against your neighbor, or do you seek to encourage and love
and help others? Are you an arrogant, or humble, person?
God resists the arrogant, but He gives grace to the humble.

Life can be good, or it can be bad. To follow the
Lord is the good life; but to follow the devil is the bad life.
Sometimes, we can fall into the hands of the devil, and it can
be a powerful grip on our lives. We can holler and scream at
him, and we can make long and loud prayers for God to take
him away from us. But, if we will not break from the
practice of sin, it is all to no avail! Praise the Lord, James

tells us how we can be free from his insidious influence and contaminating lifestyle! James 4:7-10 says:

> **"(7) Submit yourselves therefore to God. Resist the devil, and he will flee from you. (8) Draw near to God, and He will draw near to you. Cleanse your hands, you sinners, and purify your hearts, you double-minded. (9) Be penitent and mourn and weep. Let your laughter be turned to mourning and your joy to gloom. (10) Humble yourselves in the presence of the Lord, and he will exalt you."**

Ὑποτάσσω (hupotasso) is a Greek verb that means "to subject or put under." In the passive voice, it means "to become subject to," but in the middle voice, it has the force of "to obey." In the scripture before us, the word has the meaning of "to obey." The word is used 40 times in the New Testament. It is first used in Luke 2:51, when we are told that Jesus was **subject** to his parents. In Ephesians 5:21-22, we are told to **submit** ourselves to one another, and for wives likewise to **submit** to their husbands. In 1 Peter 2:13,18, we are told to **submit** to every ordinance of man and for servants to be **subject** to their masters.

The call is for us to clean our hands and to purify our hearts. The Greek word for cleanse is καθαρίσατε (katharisate), and it literally means "to wash, or cleanse the holy vessels for sacred use." It is figuratively used in a moral sense to stop using our bodies for dirty behavior and to start using our bodies as instruments of righteousness.

What does it mean to clean our hands? In the book of Romans, Paul tells us about using our bodies as instruments of righteousness. The body itself is a perfect creation of the Almighty, and, as such, is pure and holy.

However, under the influence of a polluted mind, the body can be used as an instrument of sin.

In Galatians 5:19-22, Paul vividly portrays the evil nature of the flesh. At the head of the list is the sin of πορνεία (porneia), which is sexual immorality. It is perverted sex; it is one of the blackest of sins, because it takes that which is pure and holy and makes it dirty and filthy. It is like putting nasty flies in the food we eat, or poison in the water we drink. It is taking that which is pure and holy and dragging it through the pigpen of mud and slime. It is sin that contaminates and destroys. You can dress it up with platitudes, or say that it is the natural thing to do. You can say that it is freedom to express ourselves. But, it is sin, and those who indulge in it are robbed of the precious side of marriage.

Why is it so evil? One reason is that it brings into the world children who are not wanted. It also leads to abortion, the murder of the unborn, and it brings in horrible diseases. But, most of all, it destroys the ability to really love and appreciate the opposite sex. Nothing is sweeter than for two people, a man and a woman, to come to the marriage altar and commit their lives to one another. Then, as they live in that oneness, they bring into the world children who are loved and cherished.

For three consecutive days, the Eagle newspaper ran an account of a man who had raped two college students, and tried to rape another. This is a classical example of what perverted sex can lead people into.

There is also the case of Frank King Powell, a 36-year-old man who stood condemned and looked at the floor while Judge Steven Smith read his verdict. Then, Judge Smith ordered Powel to look at the 21-year-old Blinn College student, his first victim, as she read a statement that she had prepared. She read, "That night you probably thought you had all the power in the world to take advantage of an innocent girl. But let me tell you, you may have had power for a few hours that night, but now I can say that I have power over the rest of your life." His lawyer pleaded for him, by saying that he was a family man who cares deeply for his eight children. But Powell was also reported as telling one of his victims that he raped a college-age girl every two weeks and that he had raped 20 and killed two. Powell used a gun on one of the women and a butcher knife on another one. The 36-year-old was sentenced to life in prison. This is part of the tragedy of the wages of sin. What a tragedy!

In our scripture text is also the Greek imperative, ἁγνίζω (hagnizo), which means "to morally or ceremonially make things clean." In James, we are commanded to purify our hearts. The word is used 7 times in the N.T. In the epistle of John (1 John 3:3), we are told that the hope of the resurrection **purifies** us. Peter tells us (1 Peter 1:22), "By obedience to the truth you have **purified** your souls for a sincere love for the brothers." This imperative is from the word ἅγιος (hagios), which is used 233 times, and it means "dedicated to God, holy, pure, saints, sanctuary." While the cleaning of the hands has to do with our outward actions, the purifying of our hearts is concerned about inward thoughts of the individual. As a disciple of Jesus, we are commanded to do both.

Other things that we are to abstain from are sensuality, idolatry, abuse of drugs, hostility, strife, jealousy, fits of rage, self-seeking ambition, envy, and drunkenness. Not only are we to abstain from them, we are to stop thinking about them. Whatsoever a man thinks in his heart, so is he. Our challenge is to fill our minds with good thoughts.

James called the recipients of his letter two-souled people, which meant they were double-minded. That is, they used the tongue to praise God, and with the same tongue, to curse men. They were double-minded; they were fickle. They thought they could straddle the fence, with one foot in the world and the other foot in heaven. Many people try to serve God while they are serving the flesh, but that is not possible. It must be one or the other. Light and darkness cannot dwell in the same room at the same time, because one precludes the other.

Then, we are admonished to repent, which includes mourning and weeping for the sins we have done. It is sorrow for the past behavior, but it is also an entrance into the sweet presence of the Lord. The Lord resists the self-willed and arrogant, but He gives grace to the humble. He exalts the humble and makes them sons and daughters.

We are to serve the Lord with a pure conscience. It is not our prerogative to judge our brother, but we are to encourage one another. We are not to look for faults in our brother; but, we are to look for ways we can help and encourage him/her.

We must always remember who we are. James reminds us that we are a vapor which appears for awhile and then disappears. We should never boast about who we are and what we do; but, we can say we can do this or that if it is the will of God. He can puncture our balloon anytime, but it is always a sweet privilege to walk in the shadow of His grace.

The war rages on, but we can win the battles, if we commit ourselves to Jesus our savior and commander. When the devil and his soldiers attack us, we have the power to send him and all his soldiers away in defeat. We only need to submit to God and to resist the devil, and he will leave us. When we draw near to God, He draws near to us. For victory, we cleanse our hands, and we purify our hearts. Then, the battle is won. Praise God for His deliverance!

The Works of the Flesh
(Galatians 5:16-24)

There is a difference between the godly and the ungodly, light and darkness, good and bad, and the works of the flesh and the fruit of the Spirit. The contrast between the works of the flesh and the fruit of the Spirit is vividly portrayed by the Apostle Paul in the 5th chapter of Galatians.

Paul tells the Galatians that they have been called to freedom, but that does not mean freedom to indulge in the flesh, but to serve one another in love. The whole law has been summed up in one commandment, "You shall love your neighbor as yourself." That means that we are not to be self-centered; we are not to seek to be justified by keeping the law; and, we are not to gratify the desires of the flesh.

In Galatians 5:16-24 the scripture says,

"(16) So I say, walk in the spirit and you will not gratify the lust of the flesh. (17) For the flesh lusts against the spirit and the spirit against the flesh; these are contrary to each other, to prevent you from doing what you desire. (18) But if you are led by the spirit you are not under the law. (19) The works of the flesh are obvious: fornication, uncleanness, sensuality, (20) idolatry, abuse of drugs, hostility, strife, jealousy, fits of rage, self-seeking ambition, dissensions, factions, (21) envy, drunkenness, carousing, and the like. I warn you, as I warned you before, those who do such things will not inherit the kingdom of God.

(22) But the fruit of the spirit is love,

joy,   peace,   long-suffering,   kindness,
goodness, faithfulness, (23) meekness, and
self-control.   There is no law against such
things.   (24) And those who belong to
Christ have crucified the flesh with its
passions and lusts."

We have before us the two ways of life—one way is to follow the desires of the flesh, that leads to slavery and death, and the other way is to follow the desires of the Spirit, which leads to victory and eternal life. Which way we choose to follow is the decision that each of us must make. To choose the one is to reject the other. At some point, we will examine the lifestyle of both, but today we will look at the works of the flesh.

Paul categorizes the works of the flesh into four groups. They are: (1) sensual sins, (2) idolatry and the use of drugs, (3) personal relationships, and (4) drunkenness and wild parties. Although we will be examining each of the words Paul used to describe the works of the flesh, let us examine the sensual sins first.

One of the big problems of the early church was the place of circumcision and the keeping of the law in relation to God's plan of salvation. Paul had done mighty works in the proclamation of the gospel, and many were converted and became members of the church. When the news got to Jerusalem, some of the teachers came from Judea to Antioch and taught the brethren that unless one was circumcised according to the custom of Moses, he could not be saved. This caused much discussion and discord among the church at Antioch, so they assigned Paul and Barnabas and some of the others in Antioch to go to the apostles and elders in Jerusalem concerning this problem (Acts 15:1-2).

At Jerusalem, some of the members of the church held to the position of the teachers who caused the uproar at Antioch saying, "It is necessary to circumcise the Gentiles and require them to keep the Law of Moses" (Acts 15:5). After much discussion at a conference to decide the matter, the apostles and elders at Jerusalem came up with this proclamation (Acts 15:28-29): "For it seemed good to the Holy Spirit and to us that no burden should be put on you except these necessary things: abstain from idol sacrifices, blood, from meat of strangled animals and from fornication. You will do well to keep yourselves from these things. Farewell."

You will notice that fornication is mentioned in this letter to the church in Antioch and that it is the first sin mentioned by Paul in his catalogue of the works of the flesh. It is also the first of the sins in the category of "sensual sins." The Greek word for fornication is $\pi o \rho \nu \epsilon i \alpha$ (porneia), which includes every kind of extramarital, unlawful, or unnatural sexual intercourse. The word is used 25 times in the New Testament.

When Paul wrote to the Romans, he described the awful depravity of the Romans. They had fallen so deep into the cesspool of iniquity that he wrote (Romans 1:24-28):

"(24) Therefore God gave them over in sinful desires of their hearts to sexual impurity for the degrading of their bodies with one another. (25) They exchanged the truth of God for a lie, and they worshipped and served the creature rather than the Creator, who is blessed forever. Amen.

"(26) For this reason God gave them over to shameful passions; for even their women exchanged natural intercourse for

unnatural; (27) likewise the men also, giving up natural relations with women, inflamed with passionate desire for one another, men committing shameful acts of indecency with men and receiving the wages of their own perversion. (28) They did no see fit to acknowledge God, so God gave them over to a depraved mind, to do those things which are not proper."

Some people are so depraved and have so seared their consciences that they can live in sensual sins and see no evil in it. That was the case of the Romans, for Paul said, "…and although they know the ordinance of God that those who do such things are worthy of death, and yet they not only do them, but they applaud those who practice them" (Romans 1:32). We, as a nation, are guilty of this deplorable lifestyle. But the church has a problem also, because there are many members of the institutional church who participate in this shameful lifestyle. The Bible is very plain to say that those who participate in this ungodly lifestyle have no place in the kingdom of God.

The second word ἀκαθαρσία (akatharsia), literally means "worthless material, waste; of graves, decayed flesh, causing ceremonial uncleanness, defilement; figuratively, moral uncleanness, impurity," which is the opposite of ἁγιασμός (hagiasmos), which means "holy living." The word suggests thoughts that are defiled with impurity, dirt, refuse, immorality, and viciousness. The New Testament used the word 10 times. In Romans 6:19 Paul writes, "For as you offered the members of your body as slaves of uncleanness and to iniquity unto iniquity, so now offer the members of your body in righteousness for sanctification." The synonyms for this word are "uncleanness, lewdness, and impurity of motives."

The next word is also an ugly word. It is ἀσέλγεια (aselgeia), which means "living without any moral restraint," such as licentiousness, sensuality, lustful indulgence. It is used 10 times. It refers to unrestrained living, even unbridled acts of indecency which shock the public. In Roman 13:13-14 Paul writes, "Let us live honorable as in the day, not in reveling and drunkenness, not in sexual promiscuity and licentiousness, not in strife and jealousy; but put on the Lord Jesus, and make no provision for the lusts of the flesh."

The second category in the works of the flesh is idolatry and the abuse of drugs. The Greek word for idolatry is εἰδωλολατρια (eidololatria), and the word for the abuse of drugs is φαρμακεία (pharmakeia). In the Bible, there is the tale (Isaiah 44:14-15) of the man who goes into the forest, cuts down a tree, carves out an image from the wood, and then he calls what he has made a god and falls down and worships it. We think that is foolish, and we say that we would never do such a thing as that. However, Paul wrote to the Colossians that covetousness is idolatry. The word for covetousness is πλεονεξία (pleonexia), which means "to have a disposition that wants more than a fair share." It is a greed that always calls out for more. Our idolatry can be dollar signs or anything that we put before God, our Creator. It may be a successful career, ball games, a loved one, or anything else that comes in between us and our relationship with our Father in heaven.

Oftentimes, idolatry is associated with φαρμακεία (pharmakia), which is the abuse of drugs. This word is used 3 times in the New Testament, where it is translated one time as "witchcraft" and two times as "sorceries."

Drugs, when used under the supervision of a godly doctor, can be a great healing power and a blessing to the nation. However, when they are promoted by ungodly drug dealers, they can be an awful plague that leads to destruction and death. We know this is true, because we often see lives being destroyed by this insidious evil.

The third category in the works of the flesh deals with personal relationships. This is expressed in the Greek word, ἔχθρα (echthra), which means "enmity, hostility, and hatred," both as an inner disposition and objective opposition. Its plural can be translated as "hostile feelings and acts of animosities, hostilities, discord, and feuds."

Another word in this category is ἔρις (eris), which means "strife, discord, and contentious disposition." Some people are capable of causing such strife among individuals.

The word, ζῆλος (zelos), is also in this category. It means "fervent of spirit," and it can be used both in a good and in a bad sense. In a good sense, it can mean "enthusiasm, ardent affection, and keen interest"; but, in a bad sense, it means "jealousy and envy." Jealousy can cause serious problems among people, even in the church. In the New Testament, the word is used 16 times, and most of the times are in a bad sense.

Another word, θῦμος (thumos), means "a violent anger that boils up and subsides again." It is a hot temper with angry outbursts. The person who is controlled by this disposition can be very destructive.

Other words in our third category which express some aspect of the works of the flesh are ἐριθεῖα (eritheia), which means "selfishness, selfish ambition, and selfish rivalry," and διχοστασία (dichostasia), meaning "standing apart, or disunity, dissensions, division within a community."

Another word, αἵρεσεις (haireseis), means "choice or opinion," but the word became associated with separatist groups who had loyalty to certain schools of thought and practice, sometimes translated as "sects, parties, or schools." Where some groups claimed status within the Christian community, the word was translated as "heretical sects, parties, or divisions." Where the teachings were contrary to established doctrine, it was translated as "heresy or false teaching." In our own day, we have witnessed many such teachers. We have the example of Jim Jones, who led his following to Guyana, South American, and led them to commit suicide when things got tough.

The last word in the third category of the works of the flesh is φθόνος (phthonos), which means "envy, or jealousy over the good success of another." The envious person does not want others to enjoy their possessions.

The fourth, and last, category of the works of the flesh is expressed by the word, μέθη (methee), which means "drunkenness and intoxication." Our English word, drunkenness, comes from Old English word for **drink** (ME drinken<OE drincan). It means "to be intoxicated with alcohol to the point of impairment of physical and mental faculties." The word, "intoxicate," more fully describes the fuller meaning of drunkenness. It comes from Latin and Greek and it has the idea of introducing a poison (ML intoxicat-, to poison; L in+toxicum, poison; from the word, toxic, Gk. toxikon, poison for arrows<toxon, bow). As the word suggests, liquor is a poison for the body and the brain. Liquor has been a plague upon man since the early days of mankind. In Proverbs 20:1 we read, "Wine is a mocker, strong drink is a brawler; and whosoever is led astray by them is not wise."

Noah found grace in the eyes of God and was faithful to build the ark, but after the flood, Noah planted a vineyard and drank the wine of the vineyard and became drunk. His sons found him naked in his tent. We do not know all that happened but something did, and it brought a curse upon his younger son, Canaan.

We are told that Lot was a righteous man, but he departed from his uncle Abraham and pitched his tent toward Sodom. Perhaps he just moved his tent in that direction a little each day. Finally, he was in Sodom, the wicked city. When Sodom was about to be destroyed, God instructed Lot to flee from Sodom. He was instructed to leave in a hurry and not to look back; however, Mrs. Lot looked back and was turned into a pillar of salt. He and his daughters went to live in a cave. His daughters wanted children, so they got Lot drunk, and one laid with her father one night, and the other laid with him the second night. Through these incestuous relationships came the Moabites and the Ammonites.

Although the word, κῶμος (komos), originally meant "a festive procession in honor of the wine god, merrymaking," in the New Testament it is always used in a bad sense. It is translated as "carousing, revelry, and excessive feasting."

The works of the flesh are always destructive and can never be redemptive. The natural man craves to be satisfied, but the spiritual man is committed to the God who created him/her. We must choose which master we will serve. If we follow the desires of our hearts, we are on the road to destruction. But we can accept Jesus and his way of life, and we can be filled with His presence and complete the time on earth in godly living and dying in victory. The choice is ours.

Thoughts, the Making of the Man

The Bible has much to say about overt sins; however, it also has much to say about the thoughts of a person, because that is the origin of sin. Two scriptures, Proverbs 23:7 and Matthew 15:1-20, address that issue very vividly. Using the KJV, the Proverbs verse states that "**Whatsoever a man thinketh in his heart, so is he**." Matthew 15:1-20, using the Wilton Translation, says:

"(1) Then some Pharisees and scribes from Jerusalem came to Jesus saying, (2) 'Why do your disciples transgress the tradition of the elders? For they do not wash their hands before they eat.'

"(3) Jesus replied, 'And why do you transgress the commandment of God for the sake of your tradition? (4) For God said, "Honor your father and your mother, and whoever insults his father or mother, let him be put to death." (5) But you say to your father or mother, "whatever you should have received from me is dedicated to God," (6) thus you claim that it is not necessary to honor your father; so you have annulled the Word of God to suit your tradition. (7) You hypocrites! Isaiah accurately prophesied about you, saying:

"(8) This people honor me with their lips, but their hearts are far from me.
(9) They vainly worship me; their teachings are the doctrines of men." '

"(10) And he called the people to him and said, 'Listen, and understand. (11) It is not what enters into the mouth that defiles the man, but the things coming out of the mouth, that defiles him.'

"(12) Then the disciples came to him and said, 'Do you know that the Pharisees who heard you were offended?'

"(13) Jesus replied, 'Every plant that my heavenly Father did not plant will be uprooted. (14) Leave them alone; they are blind leaders of the blind; if the blind leads the blind, they both will fall into a pit.'

"(15) Peter said to him, 'Explain the parable to us.'

"(16) So he said, 'Are you also still without understanding? (17) Do you not understand that everything entering into the mouth goes into the stomach and is cast out into the latrine? (18) But the things that come out of the mouth come from the heart, and that is what defiles the man. (19) For out of the heart come forth evil thoughts, murders, adulteries, fornications, thefts, false witnessing, and blasphemies. (20) These are the things which defile the man; but to eat with unwashed hands does not defile the man.' "

You are not what you think you are, but what you think, you are. You are not what your words say you are. There may be a big gap in what you say and what you really are. You may not be what your actions declare you to be.

Expediency and pressure from others may cause you to act out of character.

You are not what your reputation tells others that you are. You may be better or worse than what other people think of you. You are probably better than what some people think you are, and you are probably worse than what others think you are. If you come before a judge, he may think you are bad, but your mother will probably think you are good.

You are not what your clothes suggest who you are. Clothes never make the man. Some people dressed in rags are heavenly lights to those in darkness, and some dressed in the finest of clothing are rascals seeking to fleece the unfortunate.

You are not what you eat. You are more than a mass of atoms. In the parable of the rich farmer in Luke 12:16-21, we meet a man who looks at his big barns full of grain. He thought that he had blessings to last him for many years, and he said to his soul, "Soul, you have laid up many goods for many years, relax, eat, drink, and be merry." The grain was more than enough for himself and his livestock, but since man does not live by bread alone, God calls him a fool, if he only has bread on judgment day. The rich farmer's mistakes were that he lived for the present time, instead of eternity; that he lived for the material things, instead of the spiritual; and that he lived for himself, instead of others. God's response was, "Foolish man! This night your life is demanded from you, and who will get yours possessions?" The parable ends in the words, "So it is to those who lay up treasures for themselves but are not rich toward God" (Luke 12:21).

You are not what you think you are, but what you think, you are, because your thoughts are actually you. As the Proverbs 23:7 verse says, "***Whatsoever a man thinketh in his heart, so is he!***"

Man's greatest need is to think good thoughts. One night, the great astronomer, Kepler, spent an unusually long time on the roof of his house. On returning to his room, his wife asked him what he had been doing. He replied, "I have been thinking the thoughts of God."

The quality of a person's thoughts determines the character of the person. There are negative thoughts of fear and worry that can haunt and depress a person to such an extent that he becomes miserable and useless.

Attitudes and complexes are with us constantly. Good ones can be great companions to live with. Sir Sidney said, "They are never alone who are accompanied with noble thoughts." We are lonely when we are alone. The old adage is true, "an idle mind is the devil's workshop." However, we might be in a crowd of a thousand people and still be lonely. If we are accompanied with noble thoughts, we can rejoice and be glad, regardless of the circumstances.

But on the other hand, bad thoughts can cast us into dark shadows and deep valleys of despair. The base, ignoble thoughts of a person reveal the size and stature of that person. Little people have small, self-centered thoughts.

Big people are mature and are concerned about others, and they are able to rise above the slime of evil thoughts. Right thinking is the forerunner of good behavior. It is the prelude to words of wisdom, and it is more important than a reputation, because it is better to be a person of divine worth than to be respected by mortal man.

Good thoughts are of greater value then good clothes, because it is better to be clothed with the thoughts of goodness than to be arrayed in the finest of woolen garments! It is more desirable than food, because man's life consists of more than physical bread!

What we do and think about today is perhaps the result of what we were thinking about yesterday, and what we will be doing tomorrow will be determined by our thoughts today. So, where do you want your thoughts to take you?

Paul, of the New Testament, was a person who could live above circumstances. He could rejoice and be happy while tied to a ball and chain and guarded by a Roman soldier. Many had done Paul wrong, and he had suffered many injustices. However, he spent his time in prayer and thinking about the good things of life rather than trying to get even with the world, because he had learned the secret of lofty thinking.

The most important thing about you is your thoughts, because you, the real you, are your thoughts. So, **you may not be what you think you are, but what you think, you are.** For, **"whatsoever a man thinketh in his heart, so is he."**

The Galilean Pharisees had been critical of Jesus and his disciples concerning the plucking of grain on the Sabbath. They taught that plucking grain was reaping, and reaping was work. The disciples had plucked a little bit of grain to eat, because they were hungry; and, the Pharisees made a big deal about it.

The Jerusalem Pharisees questioned Jesus, saying, "Why do your disciples transgress the traditions of the elders? For they do not wash their hands before they eat?" The rabbinic custom of washing the hands before eating was not for hygienic purposes but was for ceremonial purposes. The binding force of the rabbis was considered to be greater than the Law itself.

Jesus was concerned about the more fundamental question of why the Pharisees were more concerned about their traditions than the word of God. Jesus said that they violated the commandment concerning providing help for parents, by saying that their money had been designated as a gift to God. By their tradition, they neglected their God-given responsibility to help their parents.

Then, Jesus said that Isaiah prophesied about them. He quoted from Isaiah, saying, "The people honor me with their lips but their hearts are far from me. They vainly worship me; their teachings are the doctrines of men."

Jesus called the people to him and said, "Listen, and understand. It is not what enters the mouth that defiles the man, but the things coming out of the mouth that defile."

The disciples told Jesus that the Pharisees were offended by what he said. Jesus replied, "Every plant that the heavenly Father did not plant will be uprooted. Leave them alone; they are blind leaders of the blind; the blind cannot lead the blind, they both will fall into a pit." The disciples of Jesus were confused about what Jesus was teaching, so they asked for an explanation.

Jesus said to them, "Do you not understand that everything entering into the mouth goes into the stomach and is cast into the latrine? But the things that come out of the mouth come forth from the heart and that is what defiles the man. For out of the heart come forth evil thoughts, murders, adulteries, fornications, thefts, false witnessing and blasphemies. These are the things which defile the man; but to eat with unwashed hands does not defile the man."

Jesus tells us that what comes out of the mouth is evil, because the source of the evil is the heart. Then, he tells us what comes out of the heart, which are evil thoughts, murders, adulteries, fornication, thefts, false witnessing and blasphemies.

The first Greek word in this list is πουηρός (poneros), which has the idea of evil thoughts and refers to that which is physically disadvantageous, bad, harmful, evil, painful, as of persons and things of little worth, useless, unprofitable, unserviceable. In a moral sense, of persons, it is characterized by ill will, evil, wickedness, maliciousness, also being a term for the devil. This is a picture of a polluted heart, which is the source of all evil.

The Greek word for murder is φόνος (phonos). It is used 9 times in the New Testament, and besides the meaning of murder and killing, Jesus took it beyond the overt act of murder. He said that we also ought not be angry with our brother. If we are abusive with him, we might end up in the "fires of Gehenna."

Jesus says that if you are offering your gift on the altar and remember that your brother has something against you, leave your gift before the altar and go first and be reconciled to your brother, then come and present your gift. So, making things right with your brother is the first order of business.

John also showed us that it is very important for us to love our brother. He says that if anyone says "I love God," but hates his brother, he is a liar. For the one who does not love his brother, whom he has seen, cannot love God whom he has not seen (1 John 4:20).

Is there something that we can do if we have hearts that are polluted with evil thoughts? Yes, I think that we can. Jesus addresses that problem in Matthew 5:21-47. Jesus said, "You have heard that it was said to the people of long ago, 'You shall not kill; and whoever kills shall be liable to the court.' But I say to you, whoever is angry with his brother is liable to the court...." Murder is an awful sin. Some people murder because of anger, some because of jealousy, and some for money; but, it is all because of a polluted heart. The answer is to ask God to forgive us as we forgive others. Then, we can seek the good of others.

The next two words in the list of evils, μοιχεία (moicheia), and πορνεία (porneia), meaning "adultery" and "fornication," respectively, are closely associated with one another. Adultery is illicit sex among married people, and fornication is any kind of immoral sexual activity, including homosexuality. In dealing with the subject of illicit sex, Jesus said, "You have heard that it was said: 'You shall not commit adultery.' But I say to you that everyone who looks upon a woman to lust for her has already committed adultery in his heart."

Are there some things that we can do to prevent us from falling into this pit of iniquity? First, we ought to court wholesome thoughts. For this we need to consider the books we read, the movies we attend, the places we go, and the people we hang out with. The Bible is a good book to read each day, and church services and Bible studies are uplifting. We should stay away from vulgar movies, bars, drinking parties, pornography, and profane people. You cannot walk through a pigpen without getting mud on your shoes.

The Greek word for theft, κλοπή (klope), is another condition of the heart that defiles. Our English word, "kleptomania," which means "the abnormal impulse to steal," is from this Greek word. God created us with the ability to work and to provide for ourselves and our families. However, there have been thieves in every generation. Jesus was crucified between two thieves. In the story of the Good Samaritan, thieves were waiting to rob the traveler from

Jerusalem to Jericho. Thieves are still here today, even in Bryan, Texas.

Another evil that we still have today, the false witness, is represented by the Greek word, ψευδομαρτυρία (pseudomarturia). In the days of Ahab and Jezebel, it was false witnesses who were hired to witness against that good man, Naboth. For their false testimonies, Naboth was taken and slain with his sons.

The last evil in our list of examples that pollute the heart, "blasphamies," is found in the Greek word, βλασφημία (blasphemia). It's meaning is "abusive speech against someone's reputation, or slander against the name of someone."

So, Jesus tells us that we are defiled by the evil thoughts that come from a polluted heart—the very essence of the individual. Thoughts tend to lead us into action, with good ones leading into heights of joy and usefulness, but insidious ones into the depths of destruction and death. When sin is crouching at our door to destroy us, we can overcome it if we commit ourselves to the Lord Jesus.

Although not in our list of evils, there is the associated problem of depression that often comes when everything does not seem to be going our way. It may rear its head under conditions such as when the rent may be due and there is no money left to pay it, when the family may be falling apart, when the members of the family may be sick, or when the car may be broken down. It may even occur when one has plenty of money, a beautiful home, and a new car. In any case, it comes to many people under a variety of circumstances. What is the answer? The doctors have a partial remedy for it, but Jesus has the solution, which is that "The just shall live by faith regardless of circumstances."

You are not what you think you are, but what you think, you are. Would you like to know who the happiest person is in the world? I think I know. I agree with William Lyon Phelps, who said, "The happiest man is he who thinks the most interesting thoughts."

So, if our thoughts are not so good, can we do anything about it? Yes, there is something we can do. The rituals, like washing of the hands, are not the answer. Jesus said that we are defiled by the evil thoughts that come from a polluted heart, which is the very essence of the man. Let us examine the result of faulty thinking in three different areas of life.

One of the Ten Commandments is: "You shall not murder." This is a sin that man has struggled with since the beginning of time. Cain killed his brother, Abel. We are not told why Cain killed Abel, but it must have been a premeditated murder, because we are told that he was angry with his brother (Genesis 4:6-10).

God warned Cain that sin was crouching at his door, ready to jump on him and devour him as a beast would destroy its prey. Cain was given the chance of ruling over it or being destroyed by it. Cain chose to go by the desires of the flesh. So, he killed his bother, Abel.

Some murderers kill for money or for some other personal gain. Others kill because of hostility or ill will. At our present time, many are killing because of their ideologies.

In the last few years, we have had many suicide attacks by religious fanatics who think that killing their foes will give them a ticket to heaven. The Army psychiatrist in the Fort Hood massacre is a case in hand. Major Hasan was charged with 13 counts of premeditated murder, and he was the cause of 29 people being injured. In the midst of his murderous attack, Dr. Hasan jumped up on a desk and shouted, "Allahu akbar!"—Arabic for "God is great!" What a contrast the religion of Islam is to the way Jesus taught us to love our enemies. Where do you want your thoughts to take you?

In the Old Testament, Ahab and Jezebel killed Naboth for his vineyard; Cain killed Abel because of his anger; David killed Uriah to cover up his crime. In today's world, Dr. Hasan killed 13 people because of his perverted ideas of religion. All these murders were the results of polluted minds.

The next area of Jesus' concern was perverted sex. In telling us about the polluted mind, he emphasized adultery and fornication. Adultery has to do with married people, and fornication has to do with single people and homosexuality. Adultery is taking something pure and holy and making it filthy and shamefully destructive. There is a beautifully compatible relationship between the sexes. Marriage is the consummation of the two, making them one. Through this consummation, new life is brought into the world. Children are wonderful blessings to the godly home.

When sex becomes a plaything, sin is crouching at the door. There is the problem of venereal diseases, and unwanted children leads to abortion and many other related problems. Perhaps, the most devastating fact in a promiscuous lifestyle is that it destroys the ability of one sex to love the other. Eros, the physical type of love, is not capable of holding a marriage together.

Jesus taught that the overt act was bad, but he also taught that the thoughts of a person can defile him/her. Jesus said, "...I say to you that everyone who looks upon a woman to lust for her has already committed adultery in his heart" (Matthew 5:28). In Paul's letter to the Galatians, he writes about the works of the flesh and the fruit of the Spirit. When he enumerates the list of the works of the flesh, fornication heads the list (Galatian 5:19). The perverted evil eye has caused destruction for many. Witness David with Bathsheba, Samson with Delilah, and Herod with Herodias! We have seen many men, even a carload of preachers, who have bit the dust because of an evil eye. Jesus said we should go to the extreme to overcome this problem. He said in Matthew 5:29, "…if your right eye causes you to stumble, pluck it out and throw it away, for it is better that one of the members of your body perish than that your whole body be thrown into hell."

Adultery and fornication are serious sins. The Scriptures plainly tell us that "Neither fornicators, nor idolaters, nor adulterers, nor effeminate, nor sodomites, nor thieves, nor the greedy, nor drunkards, nor slanderers, nor the rapacious will inherit the kingdom of God" (1 Corinthians 6:9-10).

We all live in fleshly bodies. How shall we treat them? If we follow the desires of the flesh, we will have big problems, but our bodies of flesh can be used as instruments of righteousness if we are led of the Spirit. Paul gives us the answer, saying, "So I do not run as one who loses sight of the finish line. I do not beat the air as one shadowboxing. I treat my body severely and make it my slave, lest after I have preached to others I myself should be disqualified" (1 Corinthians 9:26-27).

How does that work out in day-by-day activities? Are there things that we need to be on guard against? The things we read can be a bad influence; the movies we watch can defile our thoughts; the places we go can lead us astray; and liquor and drugs can pervert our behavior. The person who just drinks now and then, perhaps, drinks more now than then.

Paul said that he was a slave of Jesus. That is a wonderful relationship to Jesus. In that case, we only do what He will permit us to do. The person committed to Jesus will no more look at Playboy or other sinful magazines or evil computer filth. The commitment of Jesus becomes more powerful than the desire to sip the bottle. The young lady will dress modestly; the dresses will not be too short; and the front line will not be too low. Women know how to seduce men and many of them practice it with skill. Jesus has a better way.

Paul wrote to the Romans (13:14) with good advice: "...make no provision for the lusts of the flesh." We must diligently lead our bodies around as slaves, making no provision for the flesh. Witness the person going on a date, but first going by the drugstore to purchase contraceptives. And even worse than that, some parents give their daughters contraceptives to carry with them on dates. Those parents are participating with their children in their sins. Shame on them!

There is one more breakdown in character that we need to address. Witness the person whose life has become a nightmare. He/she may be miserable, even anticipating suicide, being bitter and tired of living. Depression is a part of this maladjusted life. What is wrong? Is there a way out?

Yes, there is a way out. What is needed is forgiveness, faith, and a purpose in living. We can have all three, if we will only submit ourselves to the Lord Jesus—in fact that was the purpose of his mission.

We first must have forgiveness, because it is our sins that have filled us with shame and disappointments. God wants to forgive us, but he is a righteous God, and if he forgave us *in* our sins, He would be violating His nature. When we are forgiven, we are holy, and that means that we have been forgive and our slate is wiped clean. Matthew 6:14-15 says, "For if you forgive others who trespass against you, your heavenly Father will also forgive you; but if you do not forgive others, neither will your Father forgive your trespasses."

Then, we must have faith, for the book of Hebrews tells us that we cannot please God without it. Hebrews 11:6 says, "Now without faith it is impossible to please God. For whoever comes to God must believe that he exists, and that he rewards those who seek him." When we live by faith, the circumstances are in the background. When we submit to God, we become slaves of Jesus. He gives us grace to overcome the world.

When we surrender our lives to Jesus, then we have purpose in life. We are no more selfishly concerned only for ourselves. We have a job to do. We become a member of the body of Christ that is concerned about sharing the Good News of Salvation to the whole world.

The solution to the problem is summed up by James, who says, "Submit yourselves therefore to God. Resist the devil, and he will flee from you. Draw near to God, and he will draw near to you. Cleanse your hands, you sinners, and purify your hears, you double-minded. Be penitent and mourn and weep. Let your laughter be turned to mourning and your joy to gloom. Humble yourselves in the presence of the Lord, and he will exalt you" (James 4:7-10). God's plan is simple: Submit to God, resist the devil, draw near to God, repent of sins, humble yourselves, and the Lord will exalt you!

Make your thoughts pure. Watch your step. Hang out with the right people. Read the good books. Go to the honorable places. Mark your Bible.

Make no provision for the flesh. When you go to encounter someone who may have wronged you, don't carry with you a concealed knife or brass knuckles—make no provisions for the flesh. When you go on a date, don't carry a fifth of whisky or a supply of drugs—make no provisions for the flesh. When you are sad and depressed and going to a secret place to grieve or mediate, don't carry a gun or a rope with you—make no provision for the flesh.

You are not what you think you are, but what you think, you are. ***"Whatsoever a man thinketh in his heart, so is he."*** Blessings on you.

Unconscious Influence
(John 20:3-8)

There are two kinds of influences in this world. One kind is the conscious influence, which we exert purposely to try to sway another, such as by teaching, by argument, by persuasion, by threatening, by gifts, or by promises. The other kind of influence, the unconscious influence, is the kind which flows from us even when it is unknown by us.

We make a conscious effort to influence people to do many things, but we also influence other in ways that are unnoticed, and we are influenced by forces that are unrealized by us. We see this happening in the Holy Bible. For example, we are told about the resurrection of Jesus in the twentieth chapter of John. Mary Magdalene was the first to come to the tomb on that first Easter morning. When she came to the tomb, she saw that the stone had been rolled away. With great excitement she ran to tell Simon Peter and John about the empty tomb. When they heard the news, Peter and John ran together to the tomb, but John outran Peter and arrived first, seeing the burial sheets lying there but not entering. When Simon Peter arrived, he entered the tomb and saw the burial sheets lying there and the napkin, which had been on the head of Jesus. The napkin was not lying with the sheets, but having been wrapped up, it was in another place. Then John, the one coming first to the tomb, entered, and he saw and believed (John 20:3-8).

From this we learn of influences that both John and Peter had on each other. John outran Peter, but he did not enter. When Peter got to the tomb, true to his nature, he burst in. Then John followed him into the tomb. Peter did not realize that he was influencing John to follow him and John did not realize that he was influenced by Peter. So, it is the same for us today. We Influence others unconsciously and they are being influenced by us unconsciously. What an awesome privilege and responsibility we have.

Influence is a subject of eternal implications. Not only is it important for today, but it can continue on like the waves of the sea. An example of this is found in my dear friends, Earl and Doris Varner, whom we met while I was stationed at Misawa Air Base in Misawa, Japan. They were a wonderful support for the Christian message, both to the Americans and the Japanese. Earl and Doris Varner have already gone to meet the Lord, but their son, Ron Varner, who was a teenage when we were in Japan, is now the pastor of a Baptist church in Goldsboro, North Carolina. This is what Ron has to say about his parents, "***They were both wonderful parents and devout followers of Jesus Christ. Their example to us kids still speaks to us today in so many little remembrances. We have such fond memories of growing up in the home of Earl and Doris Varner. How pleased the Lord must have been with how they lived their lives.***" What a tribute to one's parents! I last saw the Varners 45 years ago, but, Praise the Lord, they are still living in the lives of their children. What an awesome thought it is that we can bless our friends even after we have departed this earthly life!

You may recall that Cain and Abel were the sons of Adam and Eve, the first family living in the Garden of Eden. Abel's offering to God was accepted by the Lord, but Cain's offering was not. So, God spoke to Cain saying, "Why are you angry? Why is your face down cast? If you do what is right, will you not be accepted? But if you do not do what is right, sin is crouching at your door; it desires to have you, but you must master it." As we know, Cain did not master it. Cain asked Abel to go with him to the field, and there he killed his brother, Abel. The Lord then said to Cain, "What have you done? Listen! Your brother's blood cries out to me from the ground. Now you are under a curse and driven from the ground, which opened its mouth to receive your brother's blood from your hand." The sins of the fathers curse their children; but, the righteous influence of the fathers bless their children. Abel's blood cries out for vengeance; but, Abraham's mercies cry out for grace.

Unconscious influence is the influence that is unnoticed and unexpected. We seldom notice the sun, because it comes up and goes down in a daily routine. Some years ago, I talked to a man who had spent a tour of duty in the Air Force in Greenland. He said that for 3 or 4 months of the year the sun was not visible. When the sun did finally appear on the horizon, it was quite an occasion. Before it appeared to those at ground level, those in flight would see it while in the air and bring back word that they had seen the sun. Then, finally, one morning all would be able to see the sun for a few minutes. Later in the year, they would only be able to see the sun circling continually in the sky, and there would be no darkness for many days. To most of us in other parts of the world, the light of the sun influences our daily activities in ways that are often unnoticed.

The earth has no light of its own. It is the reflected light from the sun, with the earth acting as a bouncing board for its rays, that gives light to the earth. Since the earth has no light of its own, it is visible only because it reflects the light from the sun. But, without the light of the sun, we who are on the earth would be helpless. Physical light is absolutely indispensable, because without it life could not exist on the earth. The beasts of the jungle would go wild and frantic at the loss of light, the vegetables would turn pale and wilt and die, the earth would freeze and become a ball of ice, and the old wheels of industry would become motionless!

There is also a spiritual light that is no less wonderful. Jesus said, "I am the light of the world. A city set on a mountain cannot be hidden. Neither do people light a lamp and put it under a bowl (peck measuring), but on the lampstand, where it gives light to everyone in the house. Even so let your light shine before men, so that they may see your good works and give praise to your Father in heaven." What the sun is to our physical world, Jesus is to the spiritual universe. As the earth is dependent upon the sun for physical light, the children of men are dependent upon Christ for the spiritual light. Men do not have light within themselves, physically or spiritually. We are responsible for our unconscious influence only as the light that comes from Christ reflects in our moral character.

Unconscious influence is flowing constantly. It can be good or it can be bad. We can no more live without causing influence than we can stand without casting a shadow. It is inevitable; but, the kind of light that we have within influences the kind of light that we reflect, and the sentiments that we have are always being communicated to others. In order to be a positive reflection for good, we must first be able to receive the light that comes to us from the right source. Just as gravity is the power that holds the planets together, the influence of good people is the power that holds society together.

We often think that spectacular happenings are more important than silent powers. The spectacular event is readily noticed, but the other is not. For example, the hurricane is powerful and can cause devastation wherever it goes, but the power of the atmosphere can also give life. The earthquake has power to make the earth tremble, but the gravitational power holds the earth in orbit. The explosive power of the volcano can spew out thousands of square feet of lava to cover the earth for many miles, but the harnessed power of heat and light from the sun gives us the things necessary for life. Often, it is the silent, unnoticed influence that is ultimately more powerful than the one that makes a great spectacle. The shining light of the disciples of Jesus enlightens the path for the righteous to follow. Otherwise, the leaders of the blind and the blind will both fall into a ditch. We, who are the disciples of Jesus, have the awesome challenge to share the light of Jesus to a world in the darkness of sin.

Unconscious influence is more powerful than compulsory influence, which is unpopular. We do not like to be swayed by threats, and arguments cause more heat than light. In my younger days, I had many arguments, and I never won one, nor did I lose one. I have found that it is best to stay away from such activities that are so unproductive.

Involuntary influence is really what changes us. This might be more easily understood by the expression, "Monkey see, monkey do." As an illustration, there is the story about a person who drove through some tropical county. As he stopped to rest, he put his car keys on his cap and stretched out under a tree and went to sleep. When he woke up, he saw his keys in a monkey's hand and in a tree far above him. He shouted angrily at the monkey and pleaded for his keys, but the monkey only repeated the man's actions. So, a thought hit him. He took his house keys, raising them in the air, and angrily threw them on the ground. The monkey automatically followed his example, and the man happily retrieved his car keys.

In another incident, there was a man who was mowing his lawn. As he paused to raise a bottle of cool water to his lips for a break, his three-year-old son began to imitate his father's actions, but instead of water, he was holding a bottle of deadly, poisonous weed killer. Fortunately, as the father dashed the cold drink to the ground, the son followed his example.

Are we not influenced by fashion? Why did women start wearing high heels, and why did men start wearing ties? It must have started by unconscious influence, because no one would be able to consciously start a trend like that. I can imagine how painful it must be for women to tiptoe about on high heels. We have many customs that are good and some that are bad. A sparkling white wine was produced in Champagne, France, so the wine is called Champagne. Some people think that it must be drunk in order to celebrate special occasions, even in Holy Matrimony. How absurd! I have been in cocktail parties where people seemed to think that drinking was associated with having a good time! But the Bible tells us that "Wine is a mocker; strong drink is raging, and whosoever is deceived thereby is not wise" (Proverbs 20:1).

How does influence work in the home? The mother may take her children to church, but if she has no time for spiritual things, what will her children think? The father may tell his children that marriage is holy and that the marriage vow is eternal, but if he leaves their mother for another woman, what is he telling them? Which is more important, the teaching, or the example? The father may tell his son to obey and respect the law of the land. But, if he drives 80mph in a 50mph speed zone and tells his son to watch for the cops, what is he actually teaching his son?!

That day when Pa applied the razor strap to the appropriate place at the seat of my pants, he was telling me that I had better act right in church. That was conscious influence! It worked for me, because the next Sunday, and the next, and the next, even today, I remembered my Dad's teaching and acted accordingly.

When I went with Pa to the place that produced flower from wheat, that was unconscious influence. I spent that whole day with Pa, even before the sun came up and until after it went down. We traveled together in that wagon pulled by horses, just Pa and me. And when I went with Pa to the goat farm where he bought 2 goats for me, that was unconscious influence. That was indeed a red-letter day! For the most part of my first 20 years of life, his influence permeated everything I did. His life was my model. I thought he was the greatest Dad in the world, and I still do. That is why I wanted to be the kind of Pa he was, and I still do.

What will our influence be? I read about a tree similar to the Mimosa tree, which has a scent that can be smelled for a thousand miles away. Sometimes, when fishermen are lost at sea, they can sniff the air for the direction back home. Our influence may go even farther.

Everyone exerts influence. Horace Bushnell said, "If you had the seeds of pestilence in your body, you would not have a more active contagion than you have in your tempers, tastes, and principles. —Simply to be in the world, wherever you are, is to exert an influence—an influence too, compared with which mere language and persuasion are feeble." Bulwer said, "A good man does good merely by living." So, integrity is important. Jesus challenges us to be lights that are constantly shining (Matthew 5:14). He is more concerned about what we are than what we say. If you do not have that light, He offers it to you now.